WHO'S WHO IN
DICKENS

WHO'S WHO IN
DICKENS

MICHAEL POINTER

Grange
BOOKS

Published by Books and Toys
An Imprint of Grange Books PLC
The Grange
Grange Yard
London SE1 3AG

Produced by
Bison Books Ltd
Kimbolton House
117A Fulham Road
London SW3 6RL

ISBN 1-85627-654-6

Printed in China

PAGE 1: A formal portrait of
Charles Dickens (1812-70) in middle age.

PAGE 2: (clockwise from top
left) Madame Defarge from *A Tale of Two
Cities*; Claude Rains as John Jasper in *The
Mystery of Edwin Drood*; Alan Wheatley
playing Fogg from *The Pickwick Papers*;
Sybil Thorndike as Lady Dedlock in *Bleak
House*; Jean Simmons as Miss Havisham in
Great Expectations; and Ben Webster as
Grandfather Trent in *The Old Curiosity
Shop*.

PAGE 3: Part of the frontispiece to an early
edition of *Little Dorrit* with an illustration
by J Mahoney.

RIGHT: Part of a woodblock cut to illustrate
Martin Chuzzlewit.

CONTENTS

INTRODUCTION

The life of Charles Dickens is the archetypal story of a poor boy made good, rising from the lowest level and ending his life being buried in Westminster Abbey. He was born in 1812, and during the next ten years his family moved from Portsmouth to London, to Chatham, and back to London. His feckless father was unable to remain secure in a job, or to handle money, and at the age of 12 Charles was put to work in Warren's Blacking Factory, at Hungerford Stairs, off the Strand. For a bright, intelligent boy, this was a degrading experience that scarred him forever, and he was in his thirties before he could bring himself even to reveal that part of his early life.

ABOVE: The child Dickens at the blacking factory, an experience he used in *David Copperfield* (below).

After some further schooling he obtained his first proper job as clerk in a solicitor's office. He was little more than a glorified office boy, but it did add a little

ABOVE LEFT: The Dickens House Museum, London.
ABOVE: Dickens in 1852, the year *Bleak House* was published.
LEFT: The young Dickens "placing his first literary contribution in the editor's box".

more to his experience and his education. Throughout his life education was an important subject, as witness his regular and frequent support for various schemes for schools and institutional training. He continued to further his own education by learning and perfecting shorthand, so that he could become a freelance reporter, which he did when he was 17. His self-education continued in the Reading Room of the British Museum, and by the time he was 21 he had his first story published. The many pieces that followed, later collected as *Sketches by Boz*, pointed the way in which his lively imagination, coupled with an extraordinarily retentive memory, would furnish tale after tale and book after book, taking him to the heights of world fame and popularity from which he has never been dislodged.

ABOVE: Dickens at the height of his fame.
BELOW: An illustration by Phiz from *David Copperfield*.

remarkable, persuasive and unforgettable.

It has been claimed that more characters from the stories of Charles Dickens have found places in the halls of literary fame than from any other author. Certainly the readers of Dickens's works cherish a huge assemblage of memorable figures, as do many people who have never read the books, but who have come to the stories through adaptations for the stage, cinema and television screens.

Dickens has often been criticised for weaknesses in his plots, but surviving documents show that his story plans became more detailed and complex as his career progressed. Even so, writing as he did under the pressure of supplying monthly or weekly instalments while the novel was appearing in print must account for some of the imperfections in his work. Yet many of those shortcomings are overlooked by readers who are entranced by the behaviour, or conversation, or both, of particular characters. His bright, sharp delineation of the enormously wide range of people was always soundly based on his acute observation. It should be remembered that his experience of society eventually stretched from debtors in prison to the Queen, for his own father John Dickens had been in the Marshalsea Prison, and Charles himself had performed in amateur theatricals before Queen Victoria.

Dickens's journalistic experiences enabled him to set his scenes in solidly realistic backgrounds that were readily recognised by his readers. The parliamentary elections, coaching yards, court rooms, chapels, public houses and counting houses were all used in time to serve the ends of his fiction, and once *The Pickwick Papers* was well launched in 1837, he was able to detach himself from paid service to an employer, and to devote himself to the busy creation of the stories and characters that are now so well and widely known. As time passed, and his writing techniques developed, his creations became more and more

A little analysis shows that certain types of person recur in the various novels. With the basic story-telling premise of pitching good against evil, such recurrences are inevitable, but in Dickens's hands the similar types are given their own individualities, and there is rarely a feeling of repetition. Charles Dickens was fascinated by violence and murder, and consequently some of the strongest and most outstanding of his characters are to be found among the villains and evildoers. In his public readings from his own books, the brutal killing of Nancy by Bill Sikes was a frequent dramatic climax to his performance.

Sikes (from *Oliver Twist*) was in fact the major villain to appear in Dickens's works. Prior to him, the scoundrels in *The Pickwick Papers* were really rascals and rogues, as opposed to real evildoers, but after Sikes there followed such deliberately wicked personalities as John Chester and Mr Gashford (not even a Christian name there), from *Barnaby Rudge* and of course Jonas Chuzzlewit. Montague Tigg, also from *Martin Chuzzlewit*, is more of a confidence trickster, but is a swindler of such vast extremes that he probably qualifies as a villain, though hardly in the same class. Then there is that nasty piece of work Compeyson (*Great Expectations*), and the supremely evil Marquis St Evremonde (*A Tale of Two Cities*), beside whom James Carker (*Dombey and Son*) appears a mere amateur, and Rogue Riderhood (*Our Mutual Friend*) like a babe in arms.

Overlapping that category of villains is a group that is equally bad, but can be distinguished as a string of grotesques – a class of wrongdoers who are all

LEFT: Ronald Coleman as Sydney Carton, *A Tale of Two Cities*, 1935.
BELOW: *Oliver Twist*, 1948. John Howard Davies as Oliver, Robert Newton as Sikes.

exceptionally conspicuous. They start with Fagin, who was not the picaresque and amusing character now unfortunately too well known from the musical *Oliver!*, but an organiser of crime by others and an evil corrupter of youth on a large scale. Then there came the alarmingly cruel Wackford Squeers (*Nicholas Nickleby*) and the malevolent Daniel Quilp from *The Old Curiosity Shop*. To a lesser degree Flintwinch (*Little Dorrit*) belongs here too, but Uriah Heep (*David Copperfield*) seems to hover somewhere between the two categories.

ABOVE: Derek Bond as Nicholas Nickleby.
LEFT: Harry Secombe and Mark Lester in *Oliver!*, 1968.
BELOW: The Old Curiosity Shop, London.

Almost as bad as the villains, in some ways, are the hard and unyielding persons in authority, and the slave-drivers. Here one finds such as Ralph Nickleby, Mr Murdstone (*David Copperfield*) and Paul Dombey, and to a minor degree Thomas Gradgrind and Josiah Bounderby (*Hard Times*). Others who cause great harm, but who are not necessarily wholly responsible for all their actions are the highly neurotic Miss Wade (*Little Dorrit*), *Bradley Headstone (Our Mutual Friend), and John Jasper (Edwin Drood)*. The female trouble-makers tend to be more in the form of dragons of varying ferocity - Mrs Joe Gargery (*Great Expectations*) and Mrs Blackpool (*Hard Times*) being the most physically dangerous, while Mrs Sparsit, Mrs Clennam and Mrs Wilfer (*Hard Times, Little Dorrit* and *Our Mutual Friend* respectively) are perhaps the most vituperative.

Children were a favourite channel of Dickens for social comment, and his assembly of child victims is celebrated. Little Nell, Tiny Tim and Jo are probably the best known, but Paul and Florence Dombey should not be overlooked. Close to this group are the housekeeper heroines, with Agnes Wickfield, Ruth Pinch, Esther Summerson (*David Copperfield, Martin*

ABOVE: Murdstone with Clara Copperfield.
BELOW: Patrick Allen as Gradgrind, 1977.
BOTTOM: Billie Whitelaw as Madame Defarge, 1980.

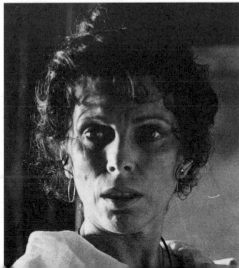

Chuzzlewit, and *Bleak House*), and of course the doyenne of them all – Little Dorrit. The generous benefactors began, naturally with Samuel Pickwick, and continued with Mr Brownlow in *Oliver Twist*, the Cheeryble brothers in *Nicholas Nickleby* and Mr Garland in *The Old Curiosity Shop*, but they seem to fizzle out as Dickens's stories become darker in character. The benefactors were often augmented by the kindly poor who assisted one another, like the Cratchits, Micawbers, Rachael, Mr Sleary, the Marchioness and Tom Pinch.

One could go on sorting, grouping and listing those delightful personages. Some do not readily fall into any easily defined class, and all are unique individuals, from Sam Weller to Durdles, from Joe to Jo, and from Arabella Allen to Rosa Bud.

About half of the great Dickens novels have the name of a character in the title, and Dickens's working papers reveal the enormous pains he took in selecting the name of a character. He had a superstitious belief in the magic of names, and would even change a character's name after he had got started. It would be an interesting exercise to ascertain the popularity of his books in proportion to the number of memorable characters therein.

TOP: Ham, *David Copperfield*, 1966.
ABOVE: John Mills as Pip in the classic 1946 *Great Expectations* and *below*, Magwitch and young Pip.

This book contains nearly four hundred of the principal characters in the major stories of Dickens. In total there are something like 1,500 different persons spread throughout his works, but many of these are little more than passing shadows on the main field of activity, and it has been felt most practical to limit the present volume to those best-known and deeply-loved persons who sprang so vividly from his rich imagination. Some that are not deeply-loved are still among the best remembered, such as the villains mentioned above. The intention is to provide a relatively easy reference to the key characters in the stories. For those seeking some of the minor and less significant people in Dickens, there are numerous encyclopaedias and reference books on Dickens that provide details falling quite outside the scope of the present work.

LEFT: David Threlfall as Smike in the RSC's production of *Nicholas Nickleby*, 1980.
BELOW: A silent *Dombey and Son*, 1917.

A

Affery

The compelled wife of Flintwinch in *Little Dorrit*. Servile to Mrs Clennam and to her husband, Affery is friendly to Arthur, and explains her marriage: "Why, if it had been a Smothering instead of a wedding, I couldn't have said a word upon it, against them two clever ones." She overhears and eavesdrops on discussions and plottings in the house, and finally rebels against Flintwinch and Mrs Clennam, in the final confrontation with Blandois. When Flintwinch absconds, she is glad to be rid of him.

Allen, Arabella

Black-eyed beauty in *The Pickwick Papers*, who captivates Nathaniel Winkle when they first meet at Dingley Dell. Her brother wishes her to marry Bob Sawyer, but this obstacle is only overcome *after* she has eloped with Winkle, when Mr Pickwick is conscripted to intervene with Benjamin Allen on Arabella's behalf. Arabella's natural charm is sufficient to persuade Mr Winkle Senior that his son is not to blame for falling in love with her. "It was your fault," he tells her, "He

Patricia Hayes as Affery and Joan Greenwood as Mrs Clennam, *Little Dorrit*.

couldn't help it." She alone, among the young ladies gathered at Manor Farm, is allowed by Dickens to show some real spirit and self-confidence.

B

Bagstock, Major Joseph
This peppery old neighbour of Miss Tox in *Dombey and Son*, is dismayed when she starts to give him the cold shoulder. He quickly perceives her designs on Mr Dombey, and pushes himself into an acquaintance with the man. Dombey is taken in by Bagstock's self-promotion, and Bagstock's plot to bring Dombey together with Edith Granger is successful. The disaster of the marriage which follows obliges Bagstock to eat his words as to his friend Dombey's importance in society.

Bailey, Benjamin
The boy at Mrs Todgers's boarding house in *Martin Chuzzlewit*. Fed up with being overworked, he leaves and becomes a smartly uniformed "tiger" to Montague Tigg at the assurance company. He is nearly killed when Tigg's carriage overturns on a stormy journey, but arrives alive and battered at the Chuzzlewits' final encounter.

Barbara
Maidservant at the home of the Garlands, in *The Old Curiosity Shop*. She and her mother become friendly with Kit and his family, and eventually she and Kit marry.

Major Bagstock advises Dombey, an illustration by Phiz.

Mrs Bardell

Bardell, Mrs

"The relict and sole executrix of a deceased custom-house officer" in *The Pickwick Papers*, "a comely woman of bustling manners and agreeable appearance". She was Mr Pickwick's landlady in Goswell Street, and "fancied she observed a species of matrimonial twinkle in the eyes of her lodger". That fancy, coupled with Pickwick's inept and blundering attempt to inform her of his intention to engage a manservant, leads to the breach of promise case for which Pickwick is tried and gaoled. Mrs Bardell's lawyers, Dodson and Fogg, not getting their costs, land her in the Fleet Prison as well, and it is her predicament that weighs with the compassionate Pickwick so that he foregoes his principles and pays to release them both.

Barkis, Mr

The somewhat dour and phlegmatic carrier in *David Copperfield*. He transports young David and his nurse Clara Peggotty between Blunderstone and Yarmouth from time to time, and on learning from David that Peggotty is unattached, sends by him one of the most restrained proposals in fiction, the message "Barkis is willin'", which sends Peggotty into hysterics. Eventually they marry, and although he professes pecuniary hardship, when he dies it becomes clear that he was not poor, and Peggotty is left well off, as is her brother Daniel.

Barnacle, Tite

A high official in the Circumlocution Office in *Little Dorrit*. He and many other members of the Barnacle family control the Circumlocution Office, the purpose of which is to prevent things being done, and to demonstrate How Not To Do It. Dickens's cynical view of the nepotism, ineptitude, idleness and financial waste of government departments is given free rein in this aspect of the book.

Barsad, John

In *A Tale of Two Cities*, an alleged gentleman, and witness at the treason trial of Charles Darnay. His evidence is largely discredited by the cross-examination of Stryver. He then appears as a police spy in the St Antoine quarter of Paris, but the Defarges have been forewarned. Cunningly, he achieves a post of responsibility under the Republican regime, but is recognised in Paris by Miss Pross as her sinful brother Solomon. This enables Sydney Carton to coerce Barsad into co-operating in his scheme to free Darnay from his condemned cell.

Bedwin, Mrs

The kindly housekeeper to Mr Brownlow in *Oliver Twist*. She quickly takes Oliver to her heart, and cannot believe that he is dishonest. Her joy at his return is tremendous: "It is my innocent boy!"

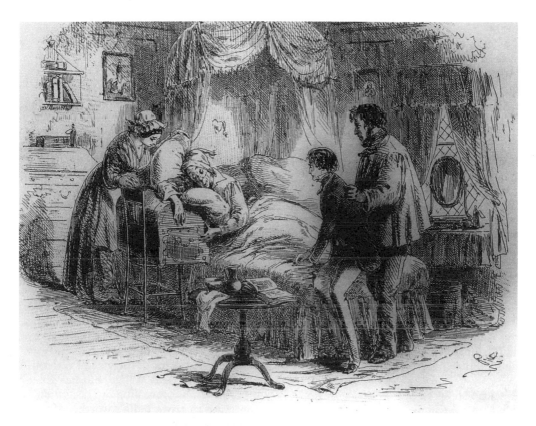

ABOVE: "Mr Barkis going out with the tide", by Phiz.
LEFT: Amy Veness as the kindly Mrs Bedwin, *Oliver Twist*, 1948.

Belle
One-time fiancée of Ebenezer Scrooge in *A Christmas Carol*. Scrooge's single-minded pursuit of wealth leads her to release him from their engagement. She is seen later as a comely matron, with a beautiful daughter and other children, and her husband reports having seen Scrooge, "quite alone in the world I believe".

Bevan, Mr
Just about the only real friend in America that Martin Chuzzlewit finds. Bevan provides a little antidote to the disagreeable features that Martin first meets, and later provides financial assistance for Martin and Mark to return to England.

Biddy

The granddaughter of Mr Wopsle's great-aunt in *Great Expectations*. She teaches Pip all she can, but sees through his pretensions to be a gentleman when he confides in her. When Mrs Joe is struck down, Biddy moves into the forge to nurse her. Although Pip cares for Biddy, he feels he has risen above her, and realises his mistake too late when he finds she has married the widowed Joe.

Bitzer

Obedient, grovelling and amazingly well-drilled pupil in the Coketown school in *Hard Times*. He gets a job as a light porter at Bounderby's bank, and quickly becomes "general spy and informer in the establishment". He colludes with the wily Mrs Sparsit, and later attempts to prevent Tom Gradgrind from escaping justice, but is frustrated by the cunning Sleary and company. Bounderby finally gives him Tom's job in the bank.

Blackpool, Mrs

A violent, uncontrollable, drunken wretch of a woman, and wife of Stephen Blackpool in *Hard Times*. She disposes of his possessions for drink, and he unsuccessfully seeks Bounderby's advice as to how to be rid of her. The angelic Rachael tends her injuries, and later, after Stephen's death, tries to help her whenever she re-appears.

Blackpool, Stephen

"A good power-loom weaver, and a man of perfect integrity" in *Hard Times*. Stephen carries a great burden of sorrows, before his tragic, wasteful death. He loves, but cannot have, the kind and gentle Rachael, because he is still married to a dissolute drunkard who steals his possessions to buy liquor. Because of a promise made to Rachael, he will not join in the trade union, and is ostracised. Unable to understand Stephen's predicament, the bombastic Bounderby discharges him, and he leaves Coketown to seek work elsewhere. When Rachael writes to tell him he is accused of robbery, he returns to clear his name, but falls into a disused mineshaft, and is fatally injured.

Blimber, Doctor

Principal of the small academy at Brighton to which Paul Dombey is transferred from Mrs Pipchin's. "The Doctor, in some partial confusion of his ideas, regarded the young gentlemen as if they were all Doctors, and were born grown up." This results in teaching methods unsuitable for the boys in his care, and Paul suffers accordingly. When the serious state of Paul's health is realised, Blimber and family treat him with extreme consideration.

Boffin, Mrs Henrietta

In *Our Mutual Friend*. "We have come into a great fortune . . . we must act up to it." Mrs Boffin is such a good-natured soul that her new riches do not greatly change her, except in the way of fashion. She is kind to Bella Wilfer, but has great difficulty in not revealing the deception contrived to prove Bella's worth.

Boffin, Nicodemus

The Golden Dustman in *Our Mutual Friend*. He is the beneficiary of a will by the late John Harmon Senior, by which he inherits the estate, including the dust heaps, following the presumed death of John Harmon Junior. The illiterate Boffin engages Silas Wegg to read to him, and Wegg conspires to relieve the kindly Boffin of his fortune. Boffin also engages John Rokesmith as his secretary, and discovers his true identity. The Boffins take into their home Bella Wilfer, who was to have married John Harmon. The apparent corruption of the Boffins by wealth drives Bella back to her own family, and she marries Rokesmith. The dismissal of Rokesmith and submission to Wegg turn out to be part of a scheme to rectify matters, and the Boffins are shown to be unspoiled after all. Boffin is based on a real-life dust contractor named Dodd, who gave his daughter as a wedding present one of his dust heaps, an unattractive gift which proved to be worth £10,000.

Bounderby, Josiah

The wealthy mill-owner and banker of Coketown in *Hard Times*. He is "a man who could never sufficiently vaunt himself a self-made man . . . the Bully of humility". The humbug Bounderby pervades the book as a horrible example of the uncaring and incorrigible brand of mill-owner that provoked employees to form combinations or unions. His marriage to Louisa Gradgrind proves a failure, and he is explosively outraged by the robbery from his bank. His pomposity is somewhat deflated when Mrs Sparsit, thinking to have secured one of the robbers, produces Bounderby's own mother, who recounts a very different version of his childhood from the gutter upbringing he has relentlessly boasted of.

Brass, Sally

In *The Old Curiosity Shop*, "a lady of thirty-five or thereabouts, of a gaunt and bony figure, and a resolute bearing, which if it repressed the softer emotions of love, and kept admirers at a distance, certainly inspired a feeling akin to awe in the breasts of those male strangers who had the happiness to approach her". She works with and dominates her brother Sampson, another of Dickens's shady lawyers, and is just as bad as him. Probably the only female in the book not afraid of Quilp, she connives in the false charge of theft against Kit Nubbles, to satisfy the grudge of Quilp, the Brasses best client.

Unabashed by the revelation of that conspiracy, she remains scornful to her accusers, taking snuff from her tin box with disdain, and slips away to send a warning note to Quilp. Her masculinity is never in doubt, even to Swiveller, who calls her "old boy."

Brass, Sampson

"An attorney of no very good repute, from Bevis Marks, in the city of London". Brass first appears, with Quilp, occupying the Old Curiosity Shop, which has fallen into Quilp's hands, but he soon returns to his own premises, where he engages Dick Swiveller, at Quilp's insistence. Always under Quilp's thumb, Brass spies on the single gentleman, who has rented the first floor, to facilitate Quilp's pursuit of Trent.

On Quilp's further instructions, Brass secures Kit's arrest on a false charge of theft, and perjures himself at the trial. Quilp's vicious treatment of Brass eventually drives him to disclose all, to his sister's great contempt, and he lands in jail.

George Ralph as Mr Bray and Jill Balcon as his unfortunate daughter, Madeleine, *Nicholas Nickleby*, 1947.

Bray, Madeline

It was one of those love-at-first-sight occurrences when Nicholas Nickleby saw Madeline at the registry office, while seeking a position. Much later he comes across her again in the Cherrybles' office. Tantalized by these fleeting glimpses, Nicholas sets Newman Noggs to follow Madeline's servant whom he sees at the office, but Noggs follows the wrong person. Then Nicholas is entrusted by the Cheerybles with conveying financial aid to the Brays, where he has his first brief interview with Madeline. Like so many of Dickens's heroines, she is pretty, meek and submissive, and steadfast to her ingrate of a father, who is later prepared to barter her in marriage to the repulsive Gride. Nicholas's endeavours to prevent that are ended when Bray collapses and dies. Madeline's fortunes are changed by the recovery of a missing will. "When her term of mourning had expired, Madeline gave her hand and fortune to Nicholas".

Bray, Walter

The father of Madeline Bray, in *Nicholas Nickleby*. This depraved parent tries to force his daughter to marry the ancient money-lender Gride, to whom he is in debt. The heartless Ralph Nickleby is the promoter of this scheme, which is only halted by the intervention of Nicholas, and Bray's sudden death.

Browdie, John

The burly, bluff, honest Yorkshire farmer in *Nicholas Nickleby*. He marries Matilda Price, a former friend of Fanny Squeers. Browdie's initial distrust of Nicholas changes to real friendship and his various acts of kindness and good deeds, culminate in his encouraging the final dissolution of the dreadful Dotheboys Hall.

Brownlow, Mr

The benevolent old gentleman who befriends Oliver Twist is one of numerous beneficent characters used by Dickens in his books to contrast with the perpetrators of crime and evil. Brownlow's trust in Oliver appears misplaced when the boy is recaptured by Fagin's gang but they are re-united by Rose Maylie, to Brownlow's immense delight. His subsequent actions in tracing Oliver's lineage and apprehending the wrongdoers result in the punishment of Fagin, Monks and the Bumbles. His adoption of Oliver at the end of the book provides a satisfactory, happy ending.

Oliver (John Howard Davies) is arrested by the chief of police (Maurice Denham), in David Lean's 1948 film, *Oliver Twist.*

Bucket, Inspector

Inspector of Detectives in *Bleak House*, initially engaged in protecting society by hounding Jo, at Tulkinghorn's behest. He is then involved in solving the murder of Tulkinghorn, and finally in preserving the status quo in society by finding Lady Dedlock for Sir Leicester.

Bud, Rosa

At first seemingly spoiled, the young and sparkling Rosa has been intended to marry Edwin Drood since childhood. Her misgivings about this arranged match lead her to a practical and sensible appraisal with Drood, who has been prompted to the same by Grewgious, and they agree to remain merely good friends. Drood's disappearance enables Jasper to make an open declaration of his love to Rosa, and she hastens to her guardian in London, Mr Grewgious, for safety.

LEFT: Rosa Bud, from *Edwin Drood*.
BELOW: "The friendly behaviour of Mr Bucket", *Bleak House*.

Bumble, Mr

Parish beadle in *Oliver Twist* who has "a great idea of his oratorical powers and his importance". Bumble has become a symbol of the oppressive ways of the old workhouse system, another target of Dickens's strong campaigning. Bumble's pomposity is matched only by his stupidity, and when married to Mrs Corney he is a deflated windbag. He allows himself to become associated with the vengeful Monks in the disposal of evidence of Oliver's true identity, yet is amazed when his misdemeanours cost him his position.

Harry Secombe as Mr Bumble and Mark Lestor as Oliver Twist, *Oliver!*, 1969.

The bullying lawyer Serjeant Buzfuz.

C

Carker, James
Second-in-command at the House of Dombey and Son. To distinguish him from his brother he is known as Mr Carker the Manager – "sly of manner, sharp of tooth, soft of foot, watchful of eye, oily of tongue, cruel of heart". Dombey, the celebrate man of business, is completely deceived by Carker, who is systematically ruining the firm. The thoroughly wicked Carker speeds the destruction of Dombey's marriage and his estrangement from his daughter Florence, by using his position of trust and influence, and employing Rob the Grinder as a spy and informer. Carker's flight to France with Edith Dombey is foiled when the miserable Rob is forced to betray their destination, and when Carker tries to escape from Dombey's pursuit he is killed in a railway accident.

Carker, John
Elder brother of James, but distinguished in the offices of Dombey and Son as Mr Carker the Junior. Past dishonesty has precluded him from further trust, and his spiteful brother ensures he is kept down and humiliated. He lives with his sister, and is kind to Walter Gay.

Carstone, Richard
A ward of John Jarndyce, and a party in the endless Chancery case. He lives at Jarndyce's home, Bleak House, with Ada Clare and Esther Summerson. He is strongly resentful of Jarndyce's cautioning to patience and restraint, as he wants to marry Ada, and to proceed with his own part of the case. That diminishes him financially, as does his inability to stick at one job and repeated sponging by Skimpole. Although he and Ada marry, they live in the shadow of the case, which gradually tells on Richard's health. The case of Jarndyce and Jarndyce collapses because the entire estate has been exhausted by costs, and Richard too succumbs, but is reconciled to Jarndyce before he dies.

Buzfuz, Serjeant
Counsel for Mrs Bardell in *The Pickwick Papers*. The bullying Buzfuz is a wicked caricature of a type of histrionic advocate frequently encountered in those and later days, and the sharp Sam Weller is the only one to make him look foolish. His bombastic manner is skilfully depicted by Dickens, and places him high in the gallery of exceptional Dickens characters, despite his relatively short appearance in the book. The many dramatisations of the Pickwick trial on stage and screen have ensured that Buzfuz is far better known (even if not by name) than would otherwise have been the case.

Carton, Sydney

In *A Tale of Two Cities*, the only bright glimmer in Carton's debauched and wasteful life is the unrequited love he develops for Lucie Manette, whom he first meets when Darnay is on trial in England. Carton puts his physical resemblance to Darnay into the hands of Stryver, who is defending Darnay, and he is acquitted. Carton is of enormous help to the ambitious Stryver by preparing cases for him, at the expense of his own health. Carton reveals his love to Lucie,

Dirk Bogarde plays Sydney Carton, 1957.

knowing it cannot be returned, and pledges himself to her service. In this novel, Dickens takes the risk of killing off Carton, the real hero of the book, at the finale of the story, and it works. The great self-sacrifice of Carton – "It is a far, far better thing that I do, than I have ever done" – contrasts pointedly with the recalling to life of Dr Manette at the beginning, and the tale, short and melodramatic, has retained its popularity.

Casby, Christopher

Landlord of the Bleeding Heart Yard in *Little Dorrit*, and father of Flora Finching. He behaves like a patriarch, but castigates Pancks for not squeezing sufficient rent from his impoverished tenants. In due time Pancks publicly exposes his false benevolence to the residents, and quits his service.

Cavaletto, John Baptist

At the beginning of *Little Dorrit* Cavaletto meets the self-styled gentleman Rigaud in a prison cell in France. Cavaletto makes his way to England, and finds a small job at the works of Doyce & Clennam. Later in the story, Arthur Clennam uses Cavaletto to find the missing Rigaud, alias Blandois, who is up to some mischief involving Clennam's mother.

Charlotte

Maid to Mrs Sowerberry, the undertaker's wife, in *Oliver Twist*. Her half-hearted efforts to shield Oliver from Noah Claypole's persecution are of little use. After Oliver's departure, she steals from Sowerberry's till, and runs off to London with Noah, where they join up with Fagin's gang.

Cheeryble, Charles

In *Nicholas Nickleby*, the Cheeryble twins, Charles and Ned, are such a prosperous, generous and virtuous pair that they are scarcely believable. Yet Dickens based them on the real-life Grant brothers of Manchester, whom he knew,

The Cheeryble brothers, *Nicholas Nickleby*.

James Hayter as Mr Cheeryble, 1947.

and he made no exaggeration. The Cheerybles are rather like a pair of Pickwicks, and their benevolence extends beyond Nicholas, whom they employ, to numerous other characters in the story. When they retire, their flourishing business is continued by their nephew Frank and Nicholas.

Cheeryble, Edwin (Ned)
See Cheeryble, Charles

Cheeryble, Frank
The robust young nephew of the Cheeryble brothers in *Nicholas Nickleby*, who assists Noggs in the apprehension of Squeers. He marries Kate Nickleby at the same time as Nicholas marries Madeline Bray.

Chester, Edward
Son of Sir John Chester in *Barnaby Rudge*. His courtship of Emma Haredale is opposed by both his father and her uncle, but the latter becomes aware of Sir John Chester's malevolent plottings, saves Emmas's life, and regrets his intervention. Edward joins with Joe Willet in rescue operations during the Gordon Riots, and receives the blessing of Emma's uncle on their union.

Chester, Sir John
In *Barnaby Rudge*, the unscrupulous father of Edward Chester, whose wish to marry Emma Haredale he will do anything to thwart. "A smooth man of the world", in Geoffrey Haredale's words, Chester is an indolent, uncaring parent. He employs Hugh for underhand tasks, and it transpires that Hugh is his illegitimate son, whom he makes no attempt to save from the gallows. Chester's devious scheming eventually becomes apparent to Geoffrey Haredale, who kills him in a duel.

Chick, Louisa
Sister to Paul Dombey Senior in *Dombey and Son*. A remarkable contrast to her cold, inflexible brother, she is addle-headed and wilfully excitable, mostly taking out her emotions on her docile husband. After encouraging her friend Lucretia Tox to think there might be a chance with her widowed brother, when Dombey marries Edith she professes huge indignation at the same idea and abandons Miss Tox. She proves incapable of the slightest understanding of the collapse of Dombey and Son.

Chivery, John
Son of the turnkey of the Marshalsea Prison, who is sweet on Little Dorrit, and becomes inconsolable when she declines his attentions. Pancks uses Chivery in his Dorrit family researches, and he later reveals to Arthur Clennam Little Dorrit's love for Arthur.

Chuffey
The pathetic old clerk who seems to live only for his master Anthony Chuzzlewit, and is oblivious to the rest of the world. Not so oblivious, however, that he does not detect Jonas in his attempt to poison his own father. Chuffey is distraught when Anthony dies, and later exposes Jonas's wickedness.

Chuzzlewit, Jonas
The evil and cruel son of Anthony Chuzzlewit in *Martin Chuzzlewit*. He

believes his plan to poison his father has succeeded, and goes to great lengths to appear a grieving and devoted son. He marries Mercy Pecksniff, and severely ill-treats her. Montague Tigg learns of the supposed crime, and coerces Jonas into investing heavily in his bogus insurance company, and into getting Pecksniff to do likewise. In desperation, Jonas murders Tigg, and is arrested for the crime. Failing to bribe himself out of arrest, he poisons himself.

Chuzzlewit, Martin, Senior

"A strong and vigorous old man, with a will of iron, and a voice of brass". A rich man also, whose wealth is coveted by a flock of relatives, in the forefront of whom is the odious cousin Pecksniff. The theme of the book is selfishness, and is proclaimed early on by old Martin himself, who is greatly troubled by everyone's attention to his wealth. His deviousness proves more than a match for that of Pecksniff, in whose home he sojourns to test Pecksniff's sincerity. In the process, both young Martin and Tom Pinch are banished by Pecksniff, but old Martin secretly sends money to Martin, and provides a job for Pinch in London.

On the day of reckoning Pecksniff is denounced, and old Martin acknowledges his own past faults in causing distress to others. "I have gratified few fancies enough in my life tending to the happiness of others, Heaven knows!"

Chuzzlewit, Martin, Junior

Grandson of old Martin, and troubled with a similar degree of selfishness. His rejection by his grandfather leads to his expedition to America, from which he returns chastened and humbled, and indebted to Mark Tapley for his life. He is a major focus of Pecksniff's actions to ingratiate himself with old Martin, and suffers accordingly. His devotion to Mary Graham is really understood by the old

Paul Scofield played both Martin and his brother Anthony Chuzzlewit in 1994.

man, and is settled on the day of reckoning when Pecksniff is finally cast out, and young Martin is openly received into his grandfather's affections. It does not seem clear to which of the two Martins the book's title refers. Perhaps Dickens intended to leave it vague.

Clare, Ada

A ward of John Jarndyce, and a party in the long-running Chancery case in *Bleak House*. Ada, Richard Carstone and Esther Summerson all become friends when they are taken to live in Jarndyce's home at Bleak House. Ada and Richard fall in love, but while she is prepared to be patient, and marry later, he chafes under any restraint. They marry in secret and live in penury. After Richard's death, she and her child live with Jarndyce.

Claypole, Noah

The surly apprentice to Mr Sowerberry, the undertaker, in *Oliver Twist*. He bullies Oliver, and his insulting references to Oliver's mother lead to Oliver's attack on him, and consequent running away. Claypole and Charlotte later rob Sowerberry and flee to London, where under the name of Morris Bolter, and by one of those amazing coincidences that abound in the book, he meets and falls in with Fagin and his gang. It is Noah who trails Nancy, discovers her rendezvous with Brownlow and Rose Maylie, and indirectly causes her death. True to type, he turns King's evidence, and becomes an informer.

Clennam, Arthur

A central and unifying character in the story of Little Dorrit. Clennam returns to England after more than 20 years in China – "exiled there until my father's death there, a year ago." The only child of strict and severe parents, there has been no love or consideration in his life and upbringing. His stern and unbending mother gives him no sort of welcome, especially as he renounces his part in the family business. He becomes interested in Little Dorrit, who does needlework for

Cly, Roger

Once a servant of Darnay in London in *A Tale of Two Cities*, he is revealed as an Old Bailey spy and false witness, whose alleged funeral causes a small riot. Jerry Cruncher is infuriated when Barsad claims to have put Cly in his coffin, and reveals his own knowledge that the contents were only paving stones and earth.

Codlin, Tom

A Punch and Judy showman in *The Old Curiosity Shop*, in partnership with Short. Codlin is the discontented grumbler, perpetually reckoning how much money the show may have lost. He and Short are convinced there is something to be gained from the mysterious grandfather and child, and Codlin repeatedly urges that he is the one who is their friend, not Short.

ABOVE: Derek Jacobi as Arthur Clennam.
RIGHT: Codlin and Short from *The Old Curiosity Shop*.
FAR RIGHT: George Jaynes as Compeyson.

his mother, and discovers her abode and family. Clennam's affectionate protection of her leads to romance, long felt by Little Dorrit, but unrecognised by him. When his business speculation fails, he is put in the Marshalsea Prison, where Little Dorrit finds and cares for him until his release, when they marry.

Clennam, Mrs

At her first appearance in *Little Dorrit*, she is the widowed and invalid mother of Arthur, and controller of the English end of the family business. A sanctimonious and inflexible tyrant, she has actually taken Arthur as her own son, after her husband fathered him by another woman. The power thus acquired over her husband enables her to pursue her unyielding and unforgiving life until Blandois tries to blackmail her with evidence of that long-hidden secret. In acute remorse, she struggles to Little Dorrit to reveal to her, but not Arthur, the sordid story.

Compeyson

In *Great Expectations*, he is the second convict that Pip sees on the marshes. He is Magwitch's sworn enemy, for he has been largely responsible for Magwitch's downfall. They are both transported, and when Magwitch returns to England, Compeyson betrays him to the police. In the struggle to re-arrest Magwitch, Compeyson is killed, and it turns out, by one of those many Dickensian coincidences, that Compeyson was the treacherous lover who jilted Miss Havisham, and caused her deranged behaviour.

Copperfield, Clara

The young widowed mother of David Copperfield, who falls for the blandishments of Murdstone, and marries him, to David's great misfortune. She is

one of the legion of Dickens's empty-headed and illogical females who cause distress all round them. Despite her love for David, she is quite reckless as to the consequences to him of her actions, and quite unable to withstand the domineering Murdstones' oppression of David. She bears a son by Murdstone, but both die while David is at Salem House School.

Copperfield, David

The young, innocent, and totally unworldly hero of the novel, who recounts his own story, some of the earlier part being based on Dickens's own painful childhood experiences. Young David's beloved mother is re-married to the implacable Murdstone, who sends him to the cruelly run Salem House School. When his mother dies, David is taken from school and sent to London to work at Murdstone's wine business, lodging with the Micawber family. Unable to bear the degrading occupation, he runs away to his great-aunt Betsey Trotwood, who places him in a decent school, and lodges him at Mr Wickfield's, where he meets Agnes Wickfield and Uriah Heep. Aunt Betsey pays for

ABOVE: "The friendly waiter and I", by Phiz, *David Copperfield*.
RIGHT: Francis L Sullivan as Bumble, Mary Clare as Mrs Corney, *Oliver Twist*, 1948.

David's articles as a proctor with Jorkins & Spenlow. When he meets Dora Spenlow, the daughter of his principal, he is immediately besotted, but his aunt's misfortune affects him financially, and their betrothal and marriage only occurs after her father dies and leaves her with little. By this time David has begun to earn a living from writing, but the delicate Dora dies. David gladly assists in the exposure of the detestable Uriah Heep, and the re-ordering of Mr Wickfield's affairs, as well as the recovery of Emily, and the passage of the Micawber family to Australia. After a sojourn abroad, he resumes writing, returns to England, and marries Agnes Wickfield.

"Of all my books, I like this the best," Dickens wrote, possibly because some of it was autobiographical.

Corney, Mrs

The matron of the workhouse in *Oliver Twist*. After the death of Old Sally, who tended Oliver's dying mother, she redeems a pawn ticket and acquires a locket and ring which would identify the foundling child. These she sells to Monks, who disposes of them. She marries Mr Bumble, and keeps the deflated former beadle under her thumb.

Crackit, Toby

A burglar associated with Fagin's gang in *Oliver Twist*. He collaborates with Bill Sikes in the attempt on Mrs Maylie's house, and returns to tell Fagin of the second loss of Oliver.

Cratchit, Bob

The poor downtrodden clerk to Ebenezer Scrooge in *A Christmas Carol*, "with fifteen shillings a week, and a wife and family". The Cratchit house in Camden Town was probably based on that in Bayham Street, where the Dickens family lived when Charles was aged 11, and the

Cratchit family is happy despite its poverty. Indeed, Bob Cratchit has an almost irrepressible good nature which serves to carry him through life's adversities. He trembles when the reformed Scrooge talks of raising his salary, so accustomed is Bob to being on the underside of life.

Cratchit, Martha
Loving wife of Bob in *A Christmas Carol*. She is the epitome of the good, homely housewives and mothers that people the stories of Dickens in the ranks of his "Kindly Poor". The only time her calm is disturbed is when Bob proposes Scrooge's health.

Cratchit, Peter

Eldest of the Cratchit children in *A Christmas Carol*. Peter is attired in one of his father's collars, and lives in hope of attaining a situation which Bob is looking out for, "which would bring in, if obtained, full five and sixpence weekly".

Cratchit, Tiny Tim

In *A Christmas Carol*, Tim must be the best-known disabled character in literature, and is the pivotal figure in the story. "Alas . . . he bore a little crutch, and had his limbs supported by an iron frame." He is often carried on the shoulders of his father, whose concern for him reaches even Scrooge's flinty heart.

Creakle, Mr

The schoolmaster at Salem House school in *David Copperfield*, and "the sternest and most severe of masters". Creakle is a vicious, child-beating brand of head teacher, who lashes out at all the boys except the favoured Steerforth. Retired from the school, he re-surfaces years later

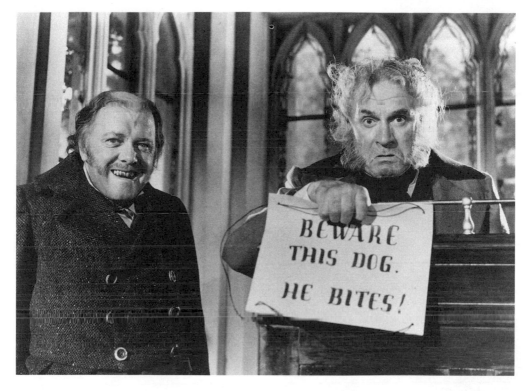

as a magistrate involved in a supposed model prison which is full of alleged repentant criminals such as the evil Heep and Littimer.

Crimple, David
Pawnbroker in *Martin Chuzzlewit*, who later is discovered in league with Montague Tigg as the Secretary of the Anglo Bengalee Disinterested Loan and Life Assurance Company. "Originally Crimp, but as the word was susceptible of an awkward construction and might be misrepresented, he had altered it to Crimple". He absconds at the time of the company's collapse.

Crisparkle, Revd. Septimus
A minor canon of Cloisterham Cathedral, in *Edwin Drood*, who lives with his mother. They take in Neville Landless for further education, and Crisparkle in concerned at Neville's fiery and ungovernable temper, but when Drood disappears, Crisparkle is not convinced of Neville's involvement, and is wary of

Jasper's vengeful wrath. He becomes allied with Grewgious in shielding the young people from Jasper's probable machinations.

Crummles, Ninetta
In *Nicholas Nickleby* better known as the Infant Phenomenon – "though of short stature, had a comparatively aged countenance, and had moreover been precisely the same age . . . certainly for five good years". She is the daughter of Vincent Crummles, who claims her to be ten years, but as "she had been kept up late every night, and put upon an unlimited allowance of gin-and-water from infancy, to prevent her from growing tall", Nicholas is understandably sceptical. Dickens allegedly based her on one Jean Davenport, a theatre manager's daughter.

ABOVE: Stanley Holloway as Vincent Crummles (1947).
RIGHT: "The Infant Phenomenon" (centre).

Crummles, Vincent

Travelling theatre proprietor in *Nicholas Nickleby*. Dickens's love of the theatre in all its aspects led him to dwell at length on the Crummles episodes of Nicholas's adventures, and the glimpses of the lives and activities of this inferior troupe of players is superb. Crummles himself recruits Nicholas and Smike to his theatrical company (who refer disrespectfully to their leader as bricks and mortar, "because his style of acting is rather in the heavy and ponderous way"). His wise choice of Nicholas for leading roles on the stage causes jealousy by the actor Lenville. The Crummleses later depart to seek success in America.

Cruncher, Jerry

Messenger for Tellson's Bank in *A Tale of Two Cities*, and part-time grave robber. He represents almost the only, if sometimes macabre, humour in the book. Jarvis Lorry uses him also as a bodyguard and takes him to Paris. The excesses of killing and butchery that he witnesses there convince him to renounce his gruesome trade, and to accept Mrs Cruncher's religious devotions for what they are.

Cruncher, Mrs

Wife of Jerry in *A Tale of Two Cities*. Nowadays she would probably be termed a battered wife. She is of a religious turn of mind, frequently flopping down on her knees, and agonising over Jerry's nocturnal activities. He intimidates her, and encourages young Jerry to do the same, blaming her praying for causing his misfortunes.

Cruncher, Young Jerry

The minder of his father's stool outisde Tellson's Bank by Temple Bar in *A Tale of Two Cities*. Young Jerry follows his father one night and discovers his other trade of grave-robbing, and later tells his father of his desire to become a Resurrection Man.

Crupp, Mrs

Landlady to David Copperfield in Buckingham Street, London. She takes advantage of the young and innocent David to swindle and short supply him, but the advent of Betsey Trotwood soon settles her and her dishonest accomplices.

Cuttle, Captain Edward

The rough, blundering old seafarer, in *Dombey and Son*, is left to hold much of the story together, after the disappearance of both Walter Gay and Sol Gills, and he provides a welcome relief from the depressing gloom of the book.

When Gills vanishes, Cuttle takes charge of his shop, and is able to receive and care for the grief-stricken Florence when she runs away from the Dombey home. This is one of only a few of his actions that turn out satisfactorily, but his kindness and loyalty are beyond question.

TOP: Captain Cuttle, *Dombey and Son*. RIGHT: Ronnie Barker as Jerry Cruncher, 1965.

D

Darnay, Charles

Nephew of the evil Marquis St Evremonde in *A Tale of Two Cities*, who sees Darnay as a traitor to the aristocracy of France by his renunciation of its despicable ways. Darnay has even taken his mother's maiden name, and lives as a tutor in London, where he marries Lucie Manette. He is lured to France by an appeal for help from Gabelle, and finds himself in prison, and condemned to death. A wooden figure, he is good at sticking to principles, but cannot grasp the impassioned enmity of the mob. He ends up owing two lives to Sydney Carton.

Christopher Sarandon as Charles Darnay, 1980.

Dartle, Rosa

Neurotic companion to Mrs Steerforth in *David Copperfield*. She bears a facial scar from a missile thrown by Steerforth, and a mental scar from her inability to ensnare him, and from his subsequent actions. She is wickedly hurtful to Emily when she is found, and her bile erupts at Mrs Steerforth when David brings the news of James's death.

Datchery, Dick

The mysterious, white-haired "old buffer" in *Edwin Drood* who arrives in Cloisterham and takes a great interest in Jasper and the alleged crime. Everything points to Datchery being another character is disguise, but his appearance in this unfinished work is too short to be of further significance.

Dedlock, Lady

The beautiful wife of the dreary Sir
Leicester is the hub of the story of *Bleak
House*. She is unaware that the
illegitimate child she had by an Army
officer is still alive, and turns out to be
Esther Summerson. At their crucial
meeting, she reveals the truth to Esther.
In the meantime both Guppy and
Tulkinghorn have discovered Lady
Dedlock's secret. Esther is able to obtain
a pledge of Guppy's silence, but
Tulkinghorn is determined to have the
truth out. After Tulkinghorn is killed,
Lady Dedlock disappears, and is sought
by Esther and Inspector Bucket, who find
her body at the gates of the cemetery
where Captain Hawdon is buried in a
pauper's grave – a site she was shown by
Jo.

Dedlock, Sir Leicester

Thick, reactionary baronet of the shires
in *Bleak House*. He is only conscious of
family honour and position in the social
scale, and is easily manipulated by
Tulkinghorn, his lawyer. Shaken by the
latter's murder, he offers a reward, but is
more shaken to learn Lady Dedlock's
secret. When he learns that this is already
known to the loathsome Smallweed and
others, it becomes too much for him, and
he suffers a fit. Still determinedly
honourable, he absolves his wife from any
blame.

Defarge, Ernest

Parisian wine shop proprietor in *A Tale of Two Cities*, and a former servant of Dr Manette, who secures the release of the doctor from the Bastille and hands him over to Jarvis Lorry and Lucie. Defarge's attitude to the family changes when he learns Lucie has married Charles Darnay, really an Evremonde, and the successor to the estate of the hated Marquis. Long a plotter for the planned revolution, he is among the leaders when the uprising occurs. His wife fears his respect for Dr Manette may weaken his resolve in eliminating all Evremondes, and she goes without him to secure Lucie and her daughter.

LEFT: Diana Rigg as Lady Dedlock, 1985
BELOW LEFT: Sir Leicester Dedlock (second left), *Bleak House* by Phiz.
BELOW: Ernest Defarge and his wife. Duncan Lamont and Rosalie Crutchley, 1957.

Defarge, Mme Therese

The wife of Ernest Defarge in *A Tale of Two Cities*, and really one of the most bitter and vindictive of all Dickens's female dragons. The secret list of those marked down for retribution is embodied in her everlasting knitting, and she spares no effort in both recording and eliminating those victims when the revolution finally comes. Boiling over with hatred, she is a natural leader of the avenging women. When Dr Manette secures the release of Darnay from the tribunal, she denounces him again on the basis of Manette's written account, found in his cell, of his treatment by the Evremondes, and she reveals that she is the sister of the girl and brother killed by the Evremondes. Determined that there shall be no survivor of that hated family, she seeks Lucie and her daughter, but is halted by the redoubtable Miss Pross. In the ensuing struggle, Therese Defarge is killed by her own pistol.

Dennis, Ned

The professional hangman in *Barnaby Rudge*, who is also an enthusiastic agitator and ringleader in the Gordon Riots. A chief reason for his "No Popery" stance seems to be that "if these Papists gets into power, and begins to boil and roast instead of hang, what becomes of my work?". His respect for constitutional law is his justification for betraying Hugh, Barnaby and Barnaby's father, but to his amazement the same law lands him in the same cell as Hugh, and both are hanged.

Deputy

The wild guttersnipe in *Edwin Drood* who is paid by Durdles to pelt him with stones to drive him home if he is out too late. Jasper is very hostile towards Deputy, and it seems that the boy may be intended as a future witness in solving the mystery.

David Copperfield arrives at his aunt's house from London. Alistair Mackenzie as David, Emlyn Williams as the simple Mr Dick, and Edith Evans, a stately Betsey Trotwood, 1969.

Dick, Mr

The seemingly foolish old man lodging at Betsey Trotwood's in *David Copperfield*. Mr Dick gives the impression of grave mental distraction by the way King Charles's head keeps obtruding in his various writings, but he shows himself capable of simple and direct solutions to problems, when consulted by Miss Trotwood, and he is repeatedly relied upon for assistance in difficult circumstances. His real name, never to be used, is Richard Babley, and Micawber manages to corrupt his adopted name to Dixon.

Dilber, Mrs

Laundress to Ebenezer Scrooge in *A Christmas Carol*. In the vision of "Yet To Come", she sells sundry items, purloined from the late Scrooge, to Joe, the scrap and junk dealer.

Diver, Colonel

Martin Chuzzlewit's first encounter with an American way of journalism is with Diver, editor of the *New York Rowdy Journal*. It marks the beginning of Martin's realisation that the way of life in America is going to be very different from what he expected. Diver introduces him to the aristocracy of dollars.

Dodger, The Artful

Real name, John Dawkins. He befriends Oliver Twist and leads him to Fagin's tender care. The Dodger is the cocky, outstanding performer in Fagin's tribe of young thieves and pickpockets, and has an inexhaustible impudence. He has been aptly referred to as a young Sam Weller turned to crime. His first outing with Oliver is a disaster, when Oliver is apprehended

Anthony Newley as the vicious Artful Dodger in David Lean's classic *Oliver Twist* of 1948.

for the Dodger's theft. Towards the end of the story the Dodger is caught and sentenced, and departs from the scene with irrepressible brazenness.

Dodson

Shady lawyer and partner of the equally shady Fogg in *The Pickwick Papers*. They encourage Mrs Bardell to proceed against Mr Pickwick, and their unscrupulous activities are well-known to Mr Perker, who regards them as very smart fellows indeed. "What a very gen'rous thing it

was o' them to have taken up the case on spec, and to charge nothing at all for costs, unless they got 'em out o' Mr Pickwick," said Sam Weller. And, of course, they did in the end.

Dombey, Florence

In *Dombey and Son*, Dickens gives us not one but two child victims: little Paul, who dies young, and Florence, who is coldly

George Cruikshank's view of the Artful Dodger.

Young and sickly Paul Dombey.

ignored by her obdurate father simply because she is not a boy. She takes refuge in the love that she and her brother have for each other, and when he dies she is left virtually neglected and friendless, except for Walter Gay, whom she regards as a substitute brother. Dombey sends Walter overseas, and he is believed drowned in a shipwreck. When her father re-marries she finds Edith very affectionate, which only alienates him further. The evil Carker continues to discredit Florence as an ally of Edith, and when he and Edith flee, Dombey is so incensed that he strikes Florence. She takes sanctuary with Captain Cuttle, at the home of Walter, who has miraculously survived his shipwreck. She and Walter marry, and go overseas. On their return she heals the breach with her ailing father, who at last is able to enjoy her love, and that of her small children.

Dombey, Paul Junior

Destined by his father to figure in the name of the House of Dombey and Son, the frail Paul has little chance of doing so, as is apparent to almost everybody but Dombey Senior. Much of the first quarter of the book is occupied with the tiny boy's tribulations, and the love and

devotion that develops between him and his sister. Despite the deep concern felt by Dombey Senior for his son, he sends him to Dr Blimber's rigorously strict school, and the boy sickens and dies under its strenuous regime. Young Paul is shrewd enough to recognise that there is no affection in his father, that Chick and Tox only pay lip-service, and that he can only rely on Florence for unselfish love. That heightens his desire for Florence to see that he is liked at Blimber's, before he is taken away to die.

Dombey, Paul Senior

Dombey and Son. "Those three words conveyed the one idea of Mr Dombey's life. The earth was made for Dombey and Son to trade in, and the sun and moon were made to give them light". His elder child, Florence, might as well not have existed, and when a son, Paul, is born, he rejoices, so far as his stern and pompous demeanour will permit. Paul's death leads him to resent Florence's survival, particularly as she and Paul were so fond of one another. Enticed by Bagstock, he meets the proud Edith Granger, and marries her as a fitting second wife. Her stubborn resistance to his imperious wishes is beyond his understanding, and their loveless marriage ends when the scheming Carker elopes with Edith. Carker has committed commercial mayhem with the family business, but Dombey is too proud and obstinate to sanction any rescue operations, and is bankrupted. This combined catastrophic retribution leaves him shattered, but an eventual reconciliation with Florence and her children is achieved.

Dorrit, Fanny

Vain, proud Fanny, who takes up dancing with the help of her selfless sister, Little Dorrit. Mrs Merdle buys her off with clothes and a bracelet when her son Sparkler becomes infatuated with her. She and her brother have their heads filled by their father with a false sense of gentility and position, and this manifests itself most despicably when the Dorrit fortune is discovered. Her ingratitude to Little Dorrit is brutal, and she is only considerate to her when it suits the maintenance of her status. She marries the hopeless Sparkler, and when the Merdle empire crashes she has to have her despised mother-in-law living with her.

LEFT: The intractable Paul Dombey Snr, by Phiz.
RIGHT: Amelda Brown as flighty Fanny Dorrit, 1987.

Dorrit, Frederick

The gentle, distracted brother of the incarcerated William Dorrit, and uncle of Little Dorrit. He plays the clarinet in a theatre orchestra until the family fortunes change, when he is persuaded by his pretentious brother to smarten his appearance and to try to be conscious of his new position in Society. He is the only one in the family who appreciates all that Little Dorrit has done for them, and he resents their offhand treatment of her when she does not fit in with their new image.

Dorrit, Little (Amy)

The small, slightly-built girl first appears to Arthur Clennam's view in the Clennam house when he returns home from China. He is fascinated by this gentle, quiet,

THESE PAGES: The highly-acclaimed film of *Little Dorrit*, 1987, with Cyril Cusack as Frederick Dorrit (right); Alec Guinness his brother William (opposite) and Ruth Pickering, Little Dorrit (below).

unobtrusive creature who does needlework for Mrs Clennam. Her abode is a mystery, and Arthur follows her to find it out. Born in the Marshalsea Prison, she has become the little mother of the Dorrit family, caring for her idle, conceited father, her wastrel brother Tip, and her socially ambitious sister Fanny. Clennam meets the family, learns some of its history, divines more, and befriends Little Dorrit, who places innocent reliance on his gentle kindness. She is fully dedicated to the care of her father, who takes her for granted, but she grows increasingly fond of Clennam. She is overwhelmed when the Dorrit fortune is discovered, and her father is released from prison, but cannot accommodate herself to the new experience of wealth, position, plenty and freedom. When her father dies, and the fortune is lost, she cares for and marries Clenman.

Dorrit, Tip

Christened Edward, the brother of Little Dorrit throws away all the opportunities provided by his sister and ends up in the Marshalsea as an imprisoned debtor like his father. Out of concern for Little Dorrit, Clennam secretly pays off his debt, but Tip's arrogant selfishness is so great that even when he learns of his obligation and pays it off, he has no appreciation of Clennam's kindness.

Dorrit, William

Father of Little Dorrit, who is born to him in the Marshalsea Prison for debtors. "A very amiable and very helpless middle-aged gentleman", he soon learns

that "the lock and key that kept him in, kept numbers of his troubles out", and he becomes resigned to the prospect of a long incarceration. In due time he is proud to be called the Father of the Marshalsea, and as such he graciously condescends to receive newcomers to the prison in his room, and comes to expect monetary gifts from those leaving the Marshalsea. His vanity increases as his sojourn in prison lengthens, and he regards as a right the financial "testimonials" given to him by the incoming and outgoing prisoners. He is sublimely oblivious of the self-sacrifice of Little Dorrit on his and the family's behalf, and when his circumstances are dramatically changed, his self-importance outweighs everything else. The family moves into Society, and in the aggrandisement of the family name he sanctions the marriage of his daughter Fanny to Edmund Sparkler, and entrusts the investment of his wealth to Edmund's stepfather Mr Merdle. Dorrit's mind is impaired, and he lapses into the belief he is still in the Marshalsea at a banquet given by Mrs Merdle. He dies a few days later.

Doyce, Daniel

The inventive engineer in *Little Dorrit*, who is unable to make progress through the impassable ways of the Circumlocution Office. With the help of Meagles, Arthur Clennam becomes his partner, and recommences the application for Doyce's invention, without success. Doyce's services are required overseas, and Clennam invests the business capital unwisely, but Doyce returns to re-establish the business.

Drood, Edwin

Nephew and ward of John Jasper, and, on the face of it, held in high affection by his uncle, which may of course be a subterfuge on Jasper's part. It remains a mystery what happens to Drood, although all the assumptions are of murder. From the little seen of him he is none too likeable – Rosa doesn't really love him, and he is largely awkward with her; he is flippant with Jasper, and insufferable towards Neville Landless – an expendable character, maybe.

Edwin Drood and Rosa Bud, *The Mystery of Edwin Drood*.

Durdles and John Jasper (Claude Rains).

Drummle, Bentley

"The next heir but one to a baronetcy" in *Great Expectations*. Drummle is a fellow student of Pip's with Matthew Pocket. Pip disliked him, and found him to be "idle, proud, niggardly, reserved, and suspicious . . . and half a dozen heads thicker than most gentlemen", and is shocked when Estella not only encourages, but marries him. Drummle treats her dreadfully, but is killed in a riding accident.

Durdles

Stone mason and eccentric custodian of the cathedral tombs in *Edwin Drood*. He is beguiled into taking Jasper round the vaults and tower at night, and claims to be able to detect the contents of sealed tombs by his tapping. He promises to take Datchery on a similar tour. Durdles pays the boy Deputy to usher him home if out too late.

E

Emily, Little

When David Copperfield first goes to Yarmouth, he meets this bright, shy girl, and is charmed by her. She is an orphan, the niece of Daniel Peggotty, in whose boat home she lives, adored by her uncle, and for long admired and then cherished by her cousin Ham. She has a long-held desire to become a lady, and elopes with the reckless Steerforth. Her assertion, "I am not as good a girl as I ought to be" proved to be true, and she pays for her waywardness when Steerforth, soon bored after the initial excitement, abandons her abroad, leaving her to be married to his manservant Littimer. She eludes him, and eventually returns to London, where her old acquaintance Martha cares for her, and leads David and Daniel Peggotty to her. Daniel takes her to Australia where they settle and prosper.

Steerforth elopes with Emily, a silent *David Copperfield*, 1913.

Endell, Martha

In *David Copperfield*, a girl who had been at school with Little Emily, and worked alongside her at Omer's haberdashery. She falls into disgrace, and is helped by Emily and Ham. When the missing Emily is being sought, Martha eventually finds her for David and Daniel Peggotty. Daniel takes her to Australia, where she marries.

Estella

Adopted daughter of Miss Havisham in *Great Expectations*. Pip finds her proud, pretty and insulting, not realising at first that Miss Havisham is bringing her up to break men's hearts, and that turns out to include his. She is educated and groomed to that end, and distresses Pip further when she marries Bentley Drummle. The only distinction she makes with men is to warn Pip off – advice he does not take. She becomes separated from her husband, who has used her with great cruelty, and fittingly, he is later killed in a riding accident. When Pip returns after 11 years abroad, they meet on the site of Satis House, her sole remaining possession.

ABOVE: Jean Simmons as the young Estella, *Great Expectations*, 1946 and *below* Pip (John Mills) and the adult Estella (Valerie Hobson) from the same film.

St Evremonde, Marquis de

In *A Tale of Two Cities*, and one of the
most wicked and evil characters in all
Dickens's work. The Marquis recognises
no moral or social responsibilities, and
treats servants and peasants as livestock
that can be killed off at will. He is
responsible for the extreme hatred shown
to the Evremonde family, and is totally
regardless of it. A callous man, he is
murdered in his bed by Gaspard, whose
child has been killed by the Marquis's
carriage.

F

Fagin

A receiver of stolen goods in *Oliver Twist*,
Fagin is also the evil organiser and keeper
of a gang of youngsters used for petty
theft. Dickens affords a glimpse of an
extraordinary facet of the Victorian
underworld which, like all his exposures,
is based on fact. The original of Fagin
was said to be one Iky Solomons, a
notorious fence of the time.

Fagin plots with Monks to discredit
and disgrace Oliver, but each time the
plans are foiled. Following Nancy's
revelations, Fagin is captured in the
round-up of the criminals (most of the
clientele of the *Three Cripples*, it seems),
and is last encountered in an eerie scene
in the condemned cell in Newgate Prison,
where he is persuaded by Mr Brownlow
and Oliver to disclose the hiding place of
the papers, given him by Monks, which
will identify Oliver.

Fan

Younger sister of Ebenezer Scrooge in *A
Christmas Carol*. Her visit to the
miserable school to bring Ebenezer home
reveals how bad the relationship between
Scrooge and his father must have been.
"Always a delicate creature", Fan dies
after bearing one child – Fred, Scrooge's
nephew.

Fang, Mr

The police magistrate before whom
Oliver Twist is taken, accused of stealing
Mr Brownlow's handkerchief. Dickens

was contemptuous of much of the legal system of his time, and his ferocious portrait of the foul-tempered Fang is an early example of his scornful treatment of such dispensers of so-called justice. Only the last-minute arrival of the bookseller saves Oliver from three months hard labour at Fang's hands.

LEFT: Oliver Reed as Sikes and Ron Moody as Fagin, *Oliver!*, 1969.
BELOW: Fagin leads his gang of young pickpockets to their hideout, *Oliver!*, 1969.

Fezziwig, Mr

In *A Christmas Carol* "an old gentleman in a Welsh wig, sitting behind such a high desk, that if he had been two inches taller he must have knocked his head against the ceiling". Scrooge and Dick Wilkins were apprenticed to Fezziwig, and enjoyed the benevolence and hospitality of that jovial man.

Finching, Flora

Daughter of Mr Casby, and one of Little Dorrit's clients for needlework. She was once a sweetheart of Arthur Clennam, before he went to China. Her husband Finching died only a few months after her marriage. Clennam finds that she has grown very broad, and short of breath, is still spoiled and artless, and talks non-stop at a breakneck speed. Dickens's former adolescent sweetheart Maria Beadnell, whom he met years later as Mrs Henry Winter, was the model for Flora, and some feel that in the ridiculous, frumpy, gushing widow with the galloping delivery, he made an unkind caricature.

Fleming, Agnes

The mysterious mother of Oliver Twist, who dies in childbirth at the parish workhouse. Much of the story is involved with the search for, and concealment of, her true identity, which is that of sister to Rose Maylie.

ABOVE: Mr Fezziwig's ball, *The Pickwick Papers*.
BELOW: The dying Agnes Fleming, Oliver Twist's mother.
RIGHT: Miriam Margolyes as Flora Finching, *Little Dorrit*.

Flintwinch, Jeremiah
In *Little Dorrit*, the cantankerous and grotesque old manager at the Clennam house, who is made a partner by Mrs Clennam when her son renounces the business. He is frequently at odds with his partner, and cruel to the wretched Affery, and while he appears to act industriously in the interests of the business, he actually steals documents which reveal much of the Clennam mystery and the wrong done to Little Dorrit. Long suspected by Arthur Clennam, he finally absconds with securities.

Folair, Mr
Pantomimist in the Crummles theatrical company in *Nicholas Nickleby*. Folair is a tale-bearing sneak and mischief maker, who conveys the conceited Lenville's note of displeasure to Nicholas.

Max Wall as the villainous Flintwinch.

Fred

Son of Fan and nephew of Ebenezer Scrooge in *A Christmas Carol*. His imperturbable good humour is placed in strong contrast with his uncle's bad temper at the beginning of the story, and it continues throughout, enabling him to welcome Ebenezer to his Christmas party with genuine sincerity.

G

Gabelle, Theophile

In *A Tale of Two Cities*, the postmaster and tax collector near the estate of the despised Marquis St Evremonde, whose bidding he is obliged to follow. Seized by the revolutionaries, he writes to Darnay for assistance on his release, causing Darnay to return to France.

Gamp, Mrs Sairey

The celebrated monthly nurse, or midwife, in *Martin Chuzzlewit*. Sairey Gamp's principal achievement, throughout her appearances in the story, is the care and comfort of herself, to the utter neglect of those in her charge. She is another of Dickens's exposures of the highly unprofessional "professionals" who were all too frequently to be found. "It was difficult to enjoy her society without becoming conscious of a smell of spirits". She was deliberately based by Dickens on a nurse who attended on the sick companion of his friend Miss Burdett Coutts, and he developed her into an outstanding character whose dialogue is a delight of verbal bedlam. He was sufficiently pleased with his creation to feature her later in his many public readings from his works. Old Martin's parting recommendation to her of "a little less liquor, and a little more humanity" sends her off in one of her walking swoons.

"Mrs Gamp has her eye on the future", by Phiz.

Gargery, Joe

The kindly, genial blacksmith in *Great Expectations*, who is married to Pip's sister. Mrs Joe leads them both a badgered existence, but they remain "ever the best of friends", and plainly enjoy each other's company very much – "What larks, Pip old chap!". Miss Havisham pays the premium for Pip's apprenticeship to Joe as a blacksmith. During the fourth year of his apprenticeship, Jaggers appears, and Pip is taken from the forge environment. Joe's subsequent visit to London is a great embarrassment to Pip, who is rapidly becoming a pseudo-gentleman. Joe remains ever the best of friends, and when Pip is lying ill, Joe cares for him, and pays his debts. Joe unwittingly spoils Pip's revised plan by marrying Biddy himself.

Bernard Miles as Joe Gargery in David Lean's *David Copperfield*.

Gargery, Mrs Joe

Sister of Pip in *Great Expectations*, and wife of Joe the blacksmith. She is one of the most ferocious of Dickens's female dragons, and leads both Pip and Joe a most uncomfortable life, using physical violence on both of them indiscriminately. "She pounced upon me" (said Pip) "like an eagle on a lamb, and my face was squeezed into wooden bowls in sinks, and my head was put under taps of waterbutts, and I was soaped, and kneaded, and towelled, and thumped, and harrowed, and rasped . . ." Totally unreasonable and illogical, she is suddenly felled by a series of dreadful blows from an intruder, and is rendered speechless and gravely handicapped "never to be on the Rampage again, while she was the wife of Joe". Her detectable nature thereafter seemed to be much more amenable, but she dies as a consequence of the injuries, and Mr Trabb organises an ostentatious funeral.

Garland, Abel
Articled clerk to the attorney Mr Witherden, in *The Old Curiosity Shop*. He is the only son of Kit's employer, and has "a quaint old-fashioned air about him, looking nearly of the same age as his father".

Garland, Mr
In *The Old Curiosity Shop*. Cast in the usual run of Dickens's benign benefactors, Mr Garland gives Kit employment at a crucial point in Kit's life, and cannot believe the accusation of Kit's dishonesty. His fat pony Whisker will only respond to control by Kit.

Gashford, Mr
In *Barnaby Rudge* there seems to be a disproportionate number of malevolents, and Gashford is one of the principals. He is the fawning secretary to Lord George Gordon, and leads and encourages his master into misjudgements with terrible consequences. "A servile, false and truckling knave", he contrives to keep himself clear of all direct responsibility for his wicked actions. Probably based by Dickens on Robert Watson, secretary to the real Lord George Gordon.

Gaspard
In *A Tale of Two Cities*, the father of the child killed by the carriage of the Marquis St Evremonde, whose callous response is typical: "It is extraordinary to me that you people cannot take care of yourselves and your children . . . How do I know what injury you have done to my horses?" Gaspard avenges himself by killing the Marquis, and when caught is hung above the fountain as an example to the villagers. This act determines the conspirators to obliterate the house of Evremonde.

Fritz Leiber as Gaspard, *A Tale of Two Cities*, 1935.

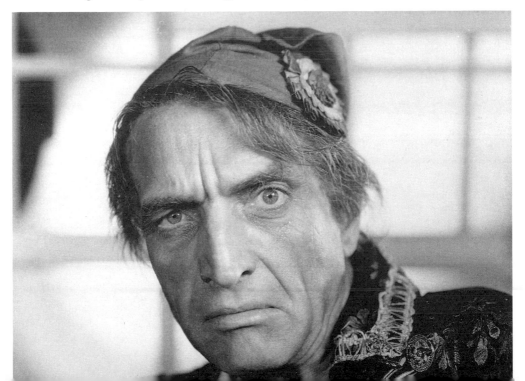

Gay, Walter

Nephew of the instrument maker Sol Gills, he is responsible for rescuing the lost young Florence. Walter is given a job in the House of Dombey and Son, and falls in love with Florence. To the great regret of his uncle, he is sent to work in the West Indies by Dombey, and is thereby missing for half of the book, which seems inappropriate for an ostensible hero of the story. Believed lost at sea, his surprise return enraptures Captain Cuttle who was acting as guardian for Florence, as well as Florence herself, and shortly afterwards she and Walter marry and depart overseas.

Walter Gay observes "the profound cogitation" of Captain Cuttle, a Phiz illustration from *Dombey and Son.*

Old Solomon Gills with Captain Cuttle, by Phiz.

General, Mrs

Employed by William Dorrit to "complete the education" of Little Dorrit and Fanny. Although she carries the air of an aristocratic lady, everything she does and says is superficial varnish, all show and no substance. Fanny hates her, and Little Dorrit is troubled by her presence.

George, Mr

Proprietor of a small shooting gallery in *Bleak House*, and an ex-sergeant who served under Captain Hawdon. Smallweed and Tulkinghorn press him to produce a specimen of Hawdon's handwriting, but he refuses until coerced by the threat of calling in the debt on his premises, which is guaranteed by a friend of his. George kindly provides a place for the dying Jo, but is arrested for the murder of Tulkinghorn. Although this is only a ruse by the wily Inspector Bucket to lull the real culprit, it brings about a reunion with George's mother, who is housekeeper at the Dedlock's home at Chesney Wold. Thus George is enabled to rejoin his family, and to attend on the enfeebled Sir Leicester.

Gills, Solomon

Instrument maker, and uncle of Walter Gay, in *Dombey and Son*. Dickens is adept at rendering helpless old characters really exasperating, and Gills is no exception. He is not only ineffectual, but takes himself off without warning or explanation when Walter is believed lost at sea, causing even more concern. But by doing so he gives place to the far more interesting Captain Cuttle.

Gordon, Lord George

He is an early example of a person from real life being used as an important character in a serious work of fiction, and in *Barnaby Rudge* the great dramatic climax of the novel is the outbreak of the so-called Gordon Riots of 1788 against Roman Catholicism.

Gordon is portrayed by Dickens as being idealistically gullible, and led by the evil Gashford deeper into sedition. His failure to foresee and understand the outcome of his activities ends in the dreadful riots, and he is placed in the Tower.

Lord George Gordon in his cell, *Barnaby Rudge*.

Gowan, Henry

In *Little Dorrit*, Gowan is resentful that his relatives in Society have done nothing for him, and trifles unconvincingly with art. He pursues and marries Minnie Meagles, and is equally resentful of her father's financial help. With this permanent chip on his shoulder, Little Dorrit perceives that he is not a person who is "in earnest".

Gradgind, Louisa

In *Hard Times*, the Gradgrind children "were all models . . . they had been lectured at from their tenderest years". With no hope of a relatively normal childhood, there is little wonder that Louisa, the eldest, submits to her dictatorial father when he brings Bounderby's proposal of marriage. She endures a loveless marriage to a man 30 years her senior with a scornful self-reliance, until it is disturbed by the carefree Harthouse. She has grown up devoid of all feelings, except towards her ungrateful brother Tom, whom she helps when he is in debt, but the unsettling effect of Harthouse's advances drives her away from both him and her impossible husband. She reveals her anguish to her father, and stays with him and Sissy. Together they clear Blackpool's name, and aid the scapegrace Tom to get out of the country.

Gradgrind, Thomas

"A man of facts and calculations" in *Hard Times*. His rigid system of utilitarian educational discipline backfires on him when his sullen son Tom becomes dissipated, and then a thief. In the meantime he has married his daughter Louisa to the tedious Bounderby, and put

Louisa Gradgrind with her ungrateful brother Tom. Jacqueline Tong and Richard Wren, *Hard Times*, 1977.

temptation in the way of the young politician Harthouse by sending him to the Bounderby home. He becomes an MP and spends much of his time in London, but fortuitously is back in Coketown when Louisa flies to him from Harthouse and Bounderby.

Gradgrind is shocked at Louisa's denunciation of her upbringing, and being fundamentally good-hearted (a condition he has not hitherto recognised), he lets her remain with him when she refuses to return to Bounderby, who fails to understand anything that is happening. Gradgrind's discomfiture is compounded when he realises his son Tom is the robber of Bounderby's bank, but he falls in with Sissy's plans to help Tom escape.

Gradgrind, Tom
Son of Thomas Gradgrind in *Hard Times*. Brought up like his sister Louisa in a rigid educational discipline, he rapidly casts it off, becoming weak-willed, dissolute and dishonest. Bounderby gives him a job in the bank. He is flattered by the friendship of Harthouse, who seeks a way to approach the emotion-proof Louisa. Heavily in debt, and unable to obtain any more money from his sister, Tom robs the bank, having first planned to incriminate Stephen Blackpool, to divert suspicion from himself. When the truth is discovered, he flees abroad, with the help of Sleary's circus, not understanding that Louisa is the only person to have loved him.

Graham, Mary
The orphan companion of old Martin Chuzzlewit, who is loved by young Martin. Her care and devotion to the old man is little acknowledged by him until the denouement, and in the meantime she has to suffer the unwelcome attentions of Pecksniff, who believes she may become a beneficiary of Chuzzlewit's will. In the end she is able to marry Martin.

Gradgrind (Patrick Allen) addresses the Coketown school.

Granger, Edith

The proud, haughty, beautiful daughter of Mrs Skewton in *Dombey and Son*. She despises her mother for the bought marriage finally secured with Dombey, and refuses to comply with her husband's demands, particularly when they are communicated through the scheming Carker. She sees in Florence an unspoiled innocent, and bestows her only affection on her, but even this is used against her, and she renounces her marriage. Coerced away by Carker, she leaves him to his fate in France. In a final act of atonement she sends a conciliatory message to Dombey through Florence.

Grewgious, Hiram

The dry, angular lawyer in *Edwin Drood*, who is the guardian of Rosa Bud, and who is curious and sceptical about the happenings at Cloisterham. For once Dickens portrays a lawyer in a sympathetic light – Grewgious acts all for the good of the parties concerned. He shrewdly divines that the long-planned match between Edwin and Rosa is not really to their liking, and stops Drood from drifting into marriage. The more he learns of Jasper and his doings, the more suspicious he becomes, and he joins Crisparkle in organising the protection of the young people.

Gride, Arthur

A repellent, aged money-lender in *Nicholas Nickleby*. Gride is helped by Ralph Nickleby to force Walter Bray (who is in debt to both of them) to compel his daughter Madeline to marry Gride. Nicholas thwarts this plan, and Gride is found to have concealed an important will, which benefits the Brays.

Grimwig, Mr

The crusty old friend of Mr Brownlow in *Oliver Twist*, who repeatedly casts doubts on Oliver's trustworthiness. "If ever that boy returns to this house, sir, I'll eat my head". Yet when Oliver is returned safely, he becomes so excited as to kiss Rose Maylie.

BELOW: "Mr Grewgious experiences a new sensation".
RIGHT: Frederick Lloyd as Mr Grimwig, *Oliver Twist*, 1948.

Grip

The raven belonging to Barnaby Rudge. He is Barnaby's only real friend, apart from his mother, and accompanies him to Newgate when Barnaby is imprisoned. He has a considerable repertoire, including the frank and often repeated "I'm a devil!". His time in prison silences him for a while, but afterwards he lives long at the Maypole farm.

Gummidge, Mrs

The widow of Daniel Peggotty's former partner in *David Copperfield*, and an unhappy resident in the Peggotty boat home. Seldom able to be other than full of self-pity, she is shaken out of her misery when she goes to Australia with Daniel and Emily, and thereafter is forever cheerful. Daniel reports: "Why, someun made offers fur to marry her!"

Guppy, William

Ambitious young solicitor's clerk in *Bleak House*. He is sharp-witted and has sufficient guile to uncover the secret of Lady Dedlock and her connection with Esther Summerson. He has already been attracted to Esther to the point of proposing, albeit unsuccessfully, but after her recovery from smallpox he changes his mind. She extracts from him a pledge never to resume his enquiries into her origins, or to disclose his knowledge. When a Jarndyce will is found that looks to conclude the interminable affair, he hastens to try once more for Esther's hand, and once more fails.

H

Haredale, Emma

Ostensibly a heroine in *Barnaby Rudge*, she actually takes very little part in the story, other than the passive one of being thwarted in love, being taken prisoner, being cared for by her Uncle Geoffrey, and being wed by Edward Chester.

Haredale, Geoffrey

Uncle to Emma in *Barnaby Rudge*. Being a Roman Catholic, he is a focus of hatred for the Gordon Rioters, and his home, The Warren, is burned down. He comes to realise that his opposition to his niece's love for Edward Chester, fomented by his father Sir John Chester, is misjudged, and he finally confronts Edward's father near the ruins of The Warren, and kills him in a duel.

Harmon, John

The beneficiary of his father's will in *Our Mutual Friend*, which requires him to marry Bella Wilfer, failing which the entire estate goes to Boffin. Harmon wanted to conceal his identity until he had formed an opinion of Bella. Following a fight, a body in the river is identified as Harmon, Boffin inherits, and Harmon changes his name to John Rokesmith. He obtains employment as Boffin's secretary, and declares his love for Bella. Newly-accustomed to living with the wealthy Boffins, she rejects him – he is only a mere secretary and lodges at her parents' house.

In time Bella values his opinion, and is dismayed by the changes in her benefactors, and their harsh treatment of Rokesmith. When Rokesmith is dismissed, she vents her anger on Boffin, and leaves the household. She and Rokesmith are soon united in a secret wedding, and set up a modest home, where they have their first child. Rokesmith is finally obliged to show his true identity, when the whole deception by the Boffins is exposed as a ruse to determine how mercenary Bella really is, and to delude Wegg in his scheming. The Boffins are happy to surrender their legacy and resume their former happy state, and they all occupy the new Boffin mansion.

Harthouse, James

Indolent young gentleman in *Hard Times*, aspiring to Parliament, and sent to Coketown to cultivate the surrounding

The duplicitous Harthouse (Edward Fox) with Louisa (Jacqueline Tong).

district to that end. To relieve his boredom, he tries to seduce Louisa, discerning that her marriage to Bounderby is an unhappy one. He cultivates her brother Tom, the only object of her affection, to work on her feelings, and succeeds in disturbing her so much that she agrees to meet him elsewhere, but goes instead to her father. Under pledge of confidentiality, Sissy Jupe obliges Harthouse to leave Coketown immediately, and never to see Louisa again.

Havisham, Miss

Miss Havisham, in *Great Expectations*, has become a celebrated character in literature – the archetypal jilted bride. She is the victim of a fraud perpetrated by her half-brother and her lover, the wretched Compeyson. When she is left in the lurch on her wedding day, she becomes deranged, and time and the environment in Satis House is made to stand still at the very minute she received the news of Compeyson's betrayal.

She seeks to wreak her vengeance on all men by bringing up the adopted Estella to torment and break men's hearts, as hers was broken. She is quite reckless as to the effect this policy will have on Pip, but otherwise treats him reasonably. After a severe altercation with Pip, she repents, and at his request bequeaths a substantial sum to Matthew Pocket, and completes the financing of Herbert's future that was begun by Pip. She is gravely burnt in a fire accident, and is saved by Pip, but succumbs to her injuries during Pip's illness. Her property is almost exclusively left to Estella.

RIGHT: Ralph Nickleby (Cedric Hardwicke) and Sir Mulberry Hawke (Cecil Ramage). BELOW: Margaret Leighton as the bitter Miss Havisham, *Great Expectations*.

Hawdon, Captain

Former lover of Honoria Barbary, and father of her illegitimate child, in *Bleak House*. Honoria eventually becomes Lady Dedlock, believing the child to be dead, and he disappears in army service. When he re-appears, years later, as an impoverished legal scribe, she chances to recognise his handwriting on a legal document used by Tulkinghorn. This causes Tulkinghorn to begin seeking a connection, but the law writer, only known as Nemo, has died from excessive use of opium. He is buried in a pauper's grave, mourned only by Jo, to whom he had been very kind.

Hawk, Sir Mulberry

A client of Ralph Nickleby's in *Nicholas Nickleby*, who is a remnant of Regency aristocratic arrogance and aggressive insolence. His clumsy advances are resisted by Kate, and his insulting references to Kate in public are overheard by Nicholas, who is so angered by Hawk's insolence that he grapples with Hawk and severely injures him. Hawk's protegé Lord Verisopht admonishes Hawk for his behaviour to Nicholas, which leads to a duel between them, and Verisopht is killed. Hawk flees to France, and on his eventual return to England he is jailed for debt.

Headstone, Bradley

Teacher in *Our Mutual Friend*, who spots talent in Charley Hexam, and helps in his further education. His contact with Charley's sister Lizzie leads him to make a proposal to her which she rejects, to Charley's dismay. Headstone accompanies Charley to Wrayburn's chambers, where Charley tries to warn Wrayburn away from his sister. Wrayburn notices Headstone's interest in Lizzie.

When Lizzie disappears, Headstone believes Wrayburn knows where she is, and constantly follows him. Wrayburn spots this, and goads Headstone by leading him all over London, night after night, reducing Headstone to grinding torments. His rage and jealousy drive him to plan Wrayburn's death, implicating Riderhood, and he almost succeeds, but for Lizzie's rescue of Wrayburn.

When Headstone learns that Lizzie is to marry Wrayburn on his sickbed, he succumbs to a fit, and gradually becomes unhinged. Riderhood tries to blackmail him, and in a final death struggle both are drowned.

Heep, Uriah

The oily and obsequious clerk to Mr Wickfield in *David Copperfield*, who so deceitfully engineers matters as to become a partner with Wickfield, until exposed and disgraced by Micawber and Traddles. His evil schemes are enveloped in a disgusting layer of false humility ("We are so very 'umble", being a constant refrain), which he retains even in his final appearance in prison. Only briefly, in the final confrontation, does his mask slip, revealing his vicious and hateful nature.

These pages: "Uriah . . . made a ghastly writhe from the waist upwards". (Below: Ron Moody as Uriah Heep.)

Hexam, Charley

Brother of Lizzie in *Our Mutual Friend*, and a thoroughly selfish and ungrateful whelp. He is helped to become a pupil teacher by Bradley Headstone, and he presses Headstone's case to Lizzie because he believes it will further his own career. He even goes to Wrayburn's chambers to tell him to desist in his attentions, without success.

He is repelled by the attack on Wrayburn, and rightly suspecting Headstone, he severs his connection with him, believing the association would damage him professionally.

Hexam, Gaffer

A river scavenger in *Our Mutual Friend*, who searches for bodies floating in the Thames. He is falsely accused of a murder, but is found drowned before the matter is cleared up.

Hexam, Lizzie

The attractive daughter of Gaffer Hexam in *Our Mutual Friend*, who rowed for her father on some of his nightly expeditions. She sends her younger brother away to school, knowing her father would not approve of his education, and when Gaffer's body is found, she moves from the waterside to live with Jenny Wren. Eugene Wrayburn, who brought her the news of Gaffer's death, is struck by her, and finds out her new address. He pays for some education for her.

Bradley Headstone, Charley's teacher, also pursues her, and to evade them both she moves again, finding work at a paper mill. Wrayburn eventually discovers her whereabouts, and rows up river to find and to see her. When he is attacked and left for dead, she uses her old skills to retrieve him from the river, and helps to nurse him. Despite his insolent ways and arrogant manners, she has become enamoured of him, and they are married in his sick room.

Hugh

Oftime friend of Barnaby Rudge, Hugh is an ostler at the Maypole inn, but becomes violently involved with the plotting and destruction of the Gordon Rioters. He is a wild, half-crazed creature, of great strength, but is captured when betrayed by Ned Dennis. He is revealed as the illegitimate son of Sir John Chester, who does nothing to save him when he is condemned to the gallows.

Hunter, Mrs Leo

Perhaps remembered chiefly for her recitations of her Ode to an Expiring Frog in *The Pickwick Papers*, she is the promoter of artistic gatherings in Eatanswill, and is the means by which Mr Pickwick encounters again the rascally Jingle, in his new guise of Charles Fitz-Marshall.

J

Jacques 1, 2 and 3 etc

In *A Tale of Two Cities* there is a rather curious and confusing method of identifying fellow conspirators for the revolution as Jacques, with a number, to protect their real names from informers and spies such as Barsad. Dickens seems not to have thought through the impracticalities of this system.

Jaggers, Mr

Guardian of Pip in *Great Expectations*, and also lawyer to Miss Havisham. This contributes to Pip's misidentification of his benefactor, a confusion that Jaggers does not help to relieve. He appears to be a bullying lawyer of the Buzfuz persuasion, but is a far deeper and more complex and interesting character. He is dependably close about all his clients' business. "I execute my instructions, and I am paid for doing so. I think them injudicious, but I am not paid for giving any opinion on their merits".

Francis L Sullivan as the dependable lawyer Jaggers, *Great Expectations*, 1935.

Jarley, Mrs

The stout and comfortable proprietress of Jarley's Waxworks in *The Old Curiosity Shop*. She behaves extremely kindly towards Nell and her grandfather, and employs Nell to exhibit the waxworks for her. Although unable to read or write, she has a refined and relatively prosperous business, and eventually marries the long-serving driver of her caravan, George.

Mrs Jarley hands the teapot to Little Nell, *The Old Curiosity Shop*.

Jarndyce, John

Owner of Bleak House, and principal
member of the family in the celebrated
Chancery case. The kind and generous
Jarndyce cares for Esther Summerson,
Ada Clare and Richard Carstone at his
home, as well as the sponger Skimpole.
In this book Dickens, never a lover of the
legal system, makes his most savage
attack on the law, particularly on the
outdated and corrupt Court of Chancery,
and this is largely done through the

Denholm Elliott as kindly John Jarndyce in
Bleak House, 1985.

mouth of Jarndyce, who declines
participation in the whole Jarndyce and
Jarndyce affair, for he is too kindly a man
to seek advantage over others from it. He
proposes to Esther, and is accepted, but
later he realises that she is in love with
Allan Woodcourt, and he gives them a
smaller version of Bleak House.

Jasper, John

The ostensible villain of the maddeningly unfinished *The Mystery of Edwin Drood*. From the very opening scene in the opium den, Jasper's behaviour is repeatedly sinister and suspicious. He takes an unusual interest in Durdles's access to the vaults and tombs in the cathedral; he inspires fear in Rosa Bud; his mulled wine given to Neville Landless and Edwin Drood appears amazingly potent, as does the liquor he gives to Durdles on their mysterious moonlight visit to the cathedral, observed by Deputy. These and other matters are all heavy hints and clues, but can this be a big red herring? Is Jasper's apparent criminality really a diversion from some other crime, which was to be divulged in the unwritten chapters?

THESE PAGES: Two saturnine portrayals of John Jasper. Left, Claude Rains in 1935, and Robert Powell in 1993, below.

Jingle, Alfred

Strolling player and general mischief maker in *The Pickwick Papers*. He is the first of Dickens's rogues, and in many ways is more of a scamp than a villain. Nowadays he would be termed a confidence trickster, or con artist, and there is an intriguing artistry in the style and manner of Jingle that only deserts

Messrs Tupman and Jingle accosted by Dr Slammer, *The Pickwick Papers*.

him when he is found incarcerated in the Fleet Prison.

His actual escapades involving the Pickwickians are worthy of being ranked with the many fictitious ones that are liberally scattered among his ceaseless anecdotes, always delivered in that peculiar telegraphese that immediately distinguishes Jingle's conversation.

In spite of his shabby appearance, and unconvincing explanations, the Pickwickians are quite taken in by this audacious rascal, Tupman even resorting to borrowing Winkle's coat for Jingle, without consent. Jingle's infiltration of the gathering at Dingley Dell results in the attempted elopement with Rachael Wardle, and, as the story proceeds, his activities become more and more outrageous.

When he re-enters the tale as a sick inmate of the Fleet Prison, we see him with a little regret at the loss of so provoking a character, as well as a little satisfaction at seeing that the scoundrel has at least received his come-uppance. A debilitated shadow of his former self, with none of his previous jauntiness, he becomes another recipient of the generosity of the soft-hearted Pickwick, and retires from the scene in uncharacteristic humility.

Jiniwin, Mrs

Mother of Betsy Quilp in *The Old Curiosity Shop*. Mrs Jiniwin is terrified of Quilp, though she tries to pretend otherwise. However, she seems to have been responsible for the marriage, for we learn that Mrs Quilp "having married the first time at her mother's instigation, she consulted in her second choice nobody but herself".

Jo

The poor, bewildered crossing sweeper in *Bleak House*. There is no respite from his persecution and distress, save when he is briefly being tended by Esther Summerson. He represents the lowest point on the social scale, of which Sir Leicester Dedlock represents the highest,

and neither would even recognise the other. Jo is full of remorse at having unwittingly infected Esther with smallpox, and apologises for it to anyone handy. His unrelieved suffering and demise are delivered by Dickens as a powerful indictment of a social system that allows homelessness and poverty to haunt the streets.

Joe

The fat boy at Dingley Dell in *The Pickwick Papers*, of whom Mr Wardle is constantly exclaiming: "Damn that boy, he's gone to sleep again". The accusation is mostly true, although there are occasions, usually to do with eating, when he is found to be very wide awake. At Rochester, at the military review, "He wasn't asleep this time, having just succeeded in abstracting a veal patty".

Most significantly, he witnesses Mr Tupman's advances to Rachael Wardle in the garden arbour. Summoned to supper, they retreat, convinced that he had seen nothing, and must have been asleep as usual. "Mr Tupman was wrong. The fat boy, for once, had not been fast asleep. He was awake – wide awake – to what had been going forward". So much so that he betrays the secret to old Mrs Wardle, and inadvertently to Jingle, thereby precipitating the disastrous attempt at elopement.

Mr Wardle might have been exaggerating when he told Pickwick that Joe "goes on errands fast asleep, and snores as he waits at table", but there is no doubting Wardle's satisfaction in having him: "I'm proud of that boy – wouldn't part with him on any account – he's a natural curiosity".

Jupe, Sissy

She is the daughter of Signor Jupe, the clown in Sleary's circus, in *Hard Times*, and is sent by her father to the school in Coketown. Her father disappears, together with his dog Merrylegs, and Gradgrind agrees to take her into his household and see that she is educated. She finds the rigid schooling exceedingly hard to understand, and through her mouth Dickens expresses much indirect criticism of some of the inflexible and inconsiderate education systems of his time. Unsurprisingly, Sissy proves a disappointment to Gradgrind who insists on using her full name, Cecilia, and goes to work in the mill, still helping in the house as well. When Louisa flees to her old home from Harthouse, Sissy takes it upon herself to banish Harthouse, and assists in Louisa's recovery. She tips off young Tom to escape when Blackpool is rescued, and sends him to Sleary's circus to hide. Gradgrind finally recognises how important she is to them all, despite her irregular start in life.

K

Kenwigs, Mr
In *Nicholas Nickleby* the Kenwigs family occupy an entire floor of the house in which Newman Noggs also has a back

Sissy Jupe (Michelle Dibnah) and Mr Gradgrind (Patrick Allen) at the circus, *Hard Times*, 1977.

garret room. Kenwigs grovels before the irascible Lillyvick, his wife's uncle, in the expectation of testamentary benefit for himself and his many children. The shock of Lillyvick's marriage turns Kenwigs against his new-born son, since he will not now be a beneficiary, but the chastened Lillyvick's return revives the family spirits tremendously, especially as Lillyvick decides to settle his money on the Kenwigs children after all.

Kenwigs, Mrs
Mother of the children whom Nicholas Nickleby is hired to teach French. "Of a delicate and genteel constitution", she manages to survive the successive catastrophes of Mr Lillyvick's marriage, desertion, and return, and to produce a baby boy into the bargain. Mr Lillyvick is her uncle; there have been high expectations of some eventual benefit from him, and in due course that turns out to be so.

Kenwigs, Morleena
Eldest of the five Kenwigs daughters in *Nicholas Nickleby*. Her uncommon Christian name "had been invented and

"There are two styles of painting; the serious and the smirk". Athene Seyler as Miss LaCreevy.

composed by Mrs Kenwigs previous to her first lying-in". Morleena artfully imitates her parents' fawning over her uncle Mr Lillyvick, in the hope of financial benefit.

Knag, Miss
Initially a supervisor of the sewing girls in Madame Mantalini's establishment in *Nicholas Nickleby*, she acquires control when the Mantalinis are bankrupted, and later joins forces with Madame to drive out the wretched Alfred.

Krook, Mr
Highly eccentric scrap dealer in *Bleak House*, who happens to have "acquired" (in lieu of back rent) a packet of letters to his lodger, the law writer. Although illiterate, Krook has enough animal cunning to piece together a few clues as to the worth of the letters, which he hides in his cat's box. He suffers the most extraordinary death in all Dickens – that of spontaneous combustion, after which Smallweed finds the letters and takes them to Tulkinghorn.

L

LaCreevy, Miss
The painter of miniature portraits in *Nicholas Nickleby*, with whom Kate and her mother lodge in London. She proves to be a true friend of the family, in spite of Mrs Nickleby's snobbish condescension, but manages to upset Mrs Nickleby greatly when she marries Tim Linkinwater.

Landless, Helena

"So womanly and handsome", is how Rosa describes her new friend in *Edwin Drood*. Helena is twin sister to Neville, but much more self-controlled, mature and amenable. She becomes instantly aware of Jasper's infatuation with Rosa, and tells her so. Rosa confides her dread of him, and they become close friends.

Landless, Neville

The hot-tempered brother of Helena is not socially experienced enough to deal with the offhand arrogance of Edwin Drood, whose uncle appears to slyly foment the dispute between them. He is accused of Drood's murder, although no body is found, and there is no case to answer, so he quits Cloisterham. Even though circumstantial evidence against him is strong, Crisparkle believes in him.

BELOW: Michelle Evans as Helena Landless, *Edwin Drood*, 1993.
RIGHT: Crisparkle (Francis L Sullivan) comforts Neville (Douglas Montgomery), 1935.

Lenville, Thomas

In the Crummles theatrical company in *Nicholas Nickleby*, he is the leading tragedian whose nose it put out of joint by the instant success of Nicholas on the stage. His vain threat to put Nicholas's nose out of joint is easily dealt with by Nicholas in one blow.

Lightwood, Mortimer

Indolent solicitor in *Our Mutual Friend*, whose only client is Mr Boffin. He shares accommodation with Eugene Wrayburn, and is appalled when he sees how Wrayburn is treating Bradley Headstone. He remains loyal to Wrayburn, helping to care for him after his attack, and becomes a busy successful lawyer working for John Harmon.

"Lightwood at Last", *Our Mutual Friend*.

Mr Linkinwater, *Nicholas Nickleby.*

Lillyvick, Mr

The pompous and short-tempered uncle
of Mrs Kenwigs in *Nicholas Nickleby*. He
is a collector of water rates, and
presumably well-off, because the
Kenwigses are blatantly obsequious in the
expectation of bequests from him. To
their dismay Lillyvick marries Miss
Petowker from the Crummles company,
but later is obliged to return and confess
to his relatives that his wife has eloped
with a half-pay captain. This leads him to
revise his monetary intentions: "Out of
affection and regard for you . . . and not
out of revenge and spite against her . . . I
shall, tomorrow morning, settle upon
your children . . . that money which I
meant to leave 'em in my will".

Linkinwater, Tim

The clerk at Cheeryble Brothers in
Nicholas Nickleby. He is fat, elderly and
large-faced, with silver spectacles and a
powdered head, and after 44 years of
service he resents the brothers' attempts
to ease his working life, but he approves
of their choice of Nicholas for the
counting-house when he has seen some of
his handiwork in the ledgers. Also, "there
sprung up quite a flirtation between Miss
LaCreevy and Tim Linkinwater", the
outcome being their betrothal and
marriage, to the lasting indignation of
Mrs Nickleby.

Littimer

The smooth, deferential, and yet intimidating manservant to Steerforth in *David Copperfield*, who is left behind in Yarmouth to facilitate the elopement of Emily with Littimer's master. When Steerforth deserts Emily abroad, she is left to be married to Littimer, but eludes him. Back in London, he is produced by Rosa Dartle to recount this to David. In a new position, he resorts to robbery, and is last seen in prison.

Lorry, Jarvis

The neat banker, dressed in brown, in *A Tale of Two Cities*, who escorts Lucie Manette to Paris to collect her father. He becomes a close friend of the family, and spends much of his time at the Manette home in Soho. He is a unifying character throughout the story, and his absences from Tellson's Bank are rather stretched to facilitate that. A self-styled "man of business", he is somewhat like a rather more efficient Pickwick, and continues working for the bank until approaching 80, when he travels to Paris to retrieve bank papers and documents from the chaos of the revolution. Thus he is on the spot when Darnay and family all arrive in the city, and is entrusted by Carton with the task of escorting them back to the safety of England.

Jarvis Lorry as portrayed by Cecil Parker, *A Tale of Two Cities*, 1958.

M

Losberne, Doctor

Surgeon and friend of the Maylies in *Oliver Twist*. He attends when Oliver is found shot, following the failed burglary, and he aids the Maylies in screening Oliver from the law. A kindly but impetuous man, he has to be restrained by Mr Brownlow so that the apprehension and interrogation of Monks can be achieved to Oliver's benefit.

Lupin, Mrs

The "comely, dimpled, plump" landlady of the Blue Dragon, where old Martin Chuzzlewit first makes his appearance. Like many in the neighbourhood, she regards Pecksniff as "such a noble-spoken gentleman", but eventually becomes aware of his hypocrisy and deceit. She is very fond of her ostler, Mark Tapley, but he leaves to be jolly elsewhere. Upon his return from America they are re-united, and soon marry.

Magnus, Peter

The ridiculously excitable, ginger-haired gentleman who presses his company on Mr Pickwick on the coach journey to Ipswich. Pickwick's accidental intrusion into the bedroom of Magnus's betrothed, Miss Witherfield, causes an upset with far-reaching consequences, being inadvertently disclosed by Winkle at the Pickwick trial.

Magwitch, Abel

The escaped convict in the churchyard on the marshes in *Great Expectations*. He pounces on young Pip, and frightens him into bringing food and a file. Together with his arch-enemy Compeyson, he is

Anthony Hopkins as Magwitch in a 1989 TV version of *Great Expectations*.

LEFT: Finlay Currie as Magwitch.
ABOVE: Peter Cushing as Dr Manette in the
1990 film of *A Tale of Two Cities*.

recaptured, and both are transported to
Australia, where Magwitch prospers and
becomes wealthy enough to repay Pip for
his assistance by making him a
gentleman; this is done through the
lawyer Jaggers, and Pip convinces himself
that his good fortune comes from Miss
Havisham.

Unable to resist seeing the results of his
generosity, Magwitch returns to England
under the name of Provis and visits Pip,
who is astounded to learn the truth.
Compeyson has detected Magwitch's
whereabouts, and Pip, now mindful of

the love Magwitch has shown him, tries
to help him to escape abroad. He is
recaptured, and dies, unaware that in the
end Pip does not receive the wealth
intended for him.

Manette, Alexandre

The good doctor of Beauvais in *A Tale of
Two Cities*, who is imprisoned in the
Bastille, thanks to the ruthless Marquis St
Evremonde, who is cursed by the doctor
in a document hidden in the wall of his
cell. Manette is severely affected by his
long confinement and isolation, and even
when released and taken to London, he
returns, at times of stress, to the
shoemaking work he performed in prison.
Although aware of Charles Darnay's real
identity, he consents to his marriage to
Lucie, and settles into a happy life in

Soho. When Darnay is enticed to France again and imprisoned, Manette uses his great reputation as an ill-treated prisoner of the aristocracy in the Bastille to obtain Darnay's release. He is devastated when his own testimony about the Evremondes, found in his cell, is used to re-arrest and condemn Darnay.

Manette, Lucie

The pretty golden-haired daughter of Dr Manette in *A Tale of Two Cities*. Her devotion to her rescued father is paramount, and she only agrees to marry Darnay if she can continue her care for the doctor. She recognises Carton's part in saving Darnay at his treason trial, but she is afraid of him, and is astonished at his declaration of love, which she agrees to keep secret. When Darnay is arrested in France, she travels with her father and child to Paris, foolishly endangering them all. Not outstandingly bright herself, perhaps she deserves the rather priggish Darnay as a husband. Nevertheless, the shrewd Carton falls for her.

Dr Manette (Henry B Walthall) and his daughter Lucie (Elizabeth Allan), from the 1935 *A Tale of Two Cities*.

Mantalini, Alfred

The silly, affected husband of Madame Mantalini in *Nicholas Nickleby*. His repeated attentions to young women drive his wife to distraction, and his reckless extravagance and gambling leads them deeper into debt with Ralph Nickleby and others, so that the business is made bankrupt. When his wife and Miss Knag combine forces against his feckless ways, he purports to poison himself, "having poisoned himself in private no less than six times within the last fortnight, and her not having once interfered by word or deed to save his life". The seventh attempt fails likewise, and, left to fend for himself, Mantalini ends up in prison, whence his release is paid for by a laundress who gets her money's worth by making him turn the mangle.

Mantalini, Madame

Proprietress of a fashionable dressmaking establishment near Cavendish Square in *Nicholas Nickleby*, to which Ralph Nickleby takes Kate to be employed (hours nine to nine, plus overtime when very busy). Madame Mantalini is so besotted with her wastrel of a husband that she shortly finds herself bankrupted.

Miss Knag, the workroom supervisor, acquires the business, and she and Madame "come to an amicable understanding" after Miss Knag has opened Madame's eyes to some of Alfred's misdemeanours. They jointly discard him for good.

BELOW: The feckless Alfred Mantalini (Cyril Fletcher) from *Nicholas Nickleby*, 1947.
BOTTOM: Kate Nickleby (Sally Ann Howes, far left) at Madame Mantalini's, 1947.

Markleham, Mrs

The mother of Annie Strong in *David Copperfield*, and an interfering busybody. "It's very much to be wished," observed Miss Trotwood, "that some mothers would leave their daughters alone after marriage, and not be so violently affectionate". Later, the Old Soldier, as she is known, is much reduced in influence.

Marley, Jacob

Erstwhile partner of Ebenezer Scrooge in *A Christmas Carol*. His ghost appears to Scrooge to warn him he has yet a chance and hope of escaping a similar fate to that holding Marley in torment.

Mary

The pretty servant-girl in the Nupkins household in *The Pickwick Papers*. The flirtation between Sam Weller and Mary develops into a love-match which re-emerges when Mary arrives at the Fleet Prison as the maid of the newly-wed Mrs Nathaniel Winkle. Joe, the fat boy, becomes infatuated with Mary, which merely earns him a considered kick from Sam. When Mr Pickwick offers Sam his release from service to marry Mary, Sam declines with a determination to continue serving his master that moves Pickwick greatly, and Mary eventually becomes Pickwick's housekeeper and marries Sam.

Maylie, Harry

Son of Mrs Maylie in *Oliver Twist*. He loves Rose, who refuses him because she believes that her alleged murky origins would harm his progress in the world. By the time Rose's true ancestry has been revealed, Harry has become the pastor of a village church, and is able to overcome her earlier objections.

Frank Finlay as Jacob Marley's ghost in a frightening scene from *A Christmas Carol*.

Maylie, Mrs

A lady of substantial means, she figures in *Oliver Twist* as the owner of the house which Sikes and Crackit attempt to burgle, thereby leaving a wounded Oliver to be found and cared for by Mrs Maylie and her adopted niece Rose.

Maylie, Rose

Adopted niece of Mrs Maylie, she befriends Oliver Twist when he is found wounded after the burglary attempt on Mrs Maylie's house. Rose's prolonged illness is held to be a reflection of that of Mary Hogarth, Dickens's sister-in-law, whose early death seriously affected the author. By another of the story's amazing coincidences, Rose Maylie turns out to be really Rose Fleming, sister of Agnes, Oliver's mother.

Meagles, Minnie

The beautiful young girl in *Little Dorrit*, whose parents befriend Arthur Clennam. She is enamoured of the amateur artist Henry Gowan (a distant relative of the Barnacle family), to the dismay of her parents, who repeatedly take her travelling to avoid Gowan, but the marriage takes place, to the regret also of Clennam. Minnie and her husband then live abroad, not particularly happily.

Meagles, Mr

A retired banker in *Little Dorrit*, who travels a lot, and assimilates very little. He and his family befriend Arthur Clennam while on the way through France to England. Meagles prides himself on being a practical man, and becomes exasperated when his friend Doyce's invention is caught in the paralysis of the Circumlocution Office, where he meets Clennam again. Meagles helps Clennam to a partnership with Daniel Doyce. He and his wife are concerned at their daughter's marriage to the penniless, well-connected but arrogant Henry Gowan, who severs relations with his in-laws. Meagles secures Doyce's return to England to alleviate Clennam's suffering.

Mell, Charles

The only considerate schoolteacher at
Salem House in *David Copperfield*. He is
kind to young David, but thanks to the
callous Steerforth he is discharged by the
obdurate Creakle. He re-appears in
Australia as Doctor Mell of Colonial
Salem House Grammar School.

Merdle, Mr

In *Little Dorrit*, Merdle is taken up by
Society solely because of his reputed
wealth and ability to acquire wealth.
Although he needs the approval of
Society in this pursuit, he is unable to
participate in its customary ways, for
which he is reproved by his wife. He is
said to be based on John Sadlier MP,
after whose suicide a large number of
swindles and frauds were discovered.

Merdle, Mrs

Renowned in Society in *Little Dorrit*, Mrs
Merdle rides high on the wave of
Society's acceptability, because of her
husband's reputation for making money.
Her objection to her son Sparkler's
infatuation for Fanny Dorrit disappears
when the Dorrit fortunes change and they
are able to move in to Society. She in turn
feels the pinch when Merdle's businesses
crash, and she has to put up with living
with Fanny and Sparkler.

Micawber, Mrs

In *David Copperfield*, the loyal wife of the
impecunious Wilkins Micawber, and
mother of his numerous children. Despite
their constant financial scrapes and
predicaments, she avers she will never
desert him, and frequently wishes to
know whether proposed situations have
the possibility of high advancement for
him. As things turn out, he achieves just
that, as a magistrate in Australia.

LEFT: Eleanor Bron as *Little Dorrit*'s Mrs Merdle, 1987.
BELOW LEFT: W C Fields, a classic Micawber in the 1935 film. Frank Lawton played David Copperfield.
BELOW: Mr Micawber escorts David Copperfield to his new lodgings.

Micawber, Wilkins

Young David Copperfield lodges with Micawber and his family when sent to London to work. Micawber has become famous as the perpetual debtor, constantly expecting something to turn up. What turns up in the story, often

unexpectedly, is Micawber himself, enriching the novel with his flamboyant manner and orotund observations as he evades creditor after creditor: "Annual income twenty pounds, annual expenditure nineteen nineteen six, result happiness. Annual income twenty pounds, annual expenditure twenty pounds eight and six, result misery". Micawber obtains a position with Wickfield and Heep, and becomes instrumental in exposing the fraudulent Uriah. With the help of Miss Trotwood he emigrates to Australia, where he prospers, pays off all his debts, and becomes an honoured magistrate.

Miggs, Miss

In *Barnaby Rudge* Miggs is one of Dickens's noteworthy termagents. She encourages her mistress, Mrs Varden, in temperamental behaviour, to the discomfort of Gabriel Varden, and frustrates Varden's defence of his premises against the Gordon Rioters by pouring beer down the barrel of his gun. She wants to accompany Simon Tappertit and the mob, but Simon orders her confined with Dolly and Emma, not knowing what else to do with the ceaselessly prattling shrew.

She continues her open advocacy of the riots while in captivity, and after release by Joe and Edward she has the audacity to return to the Varden's, expecting to resume her position, but Mrs Varden has seen her in her true colours, and discharges her.

Mills, Julia

A friend of Dora Spenlow, and a go-between to David Copperfield when their romance has to be kept secret. Although kind to Dora and David, when she returns from a long spell in India her only interests seem to be ultra-fashionable society, and money.

Molly

In *Great Expectations* she is the subdued and watchful housekeeper to Mr Jaggers, who is pleased to display her physical strength. Thanks to Jaggers she has been acquitted of murder, and Pip works out that she is Estella's mother, and the former partner of Magwitch.

David Copperfield (Freddie Bartholomew) confronts his new stepfather, the heartless Murdstone (Basil Rathbone), 1935.

Monks

Half-brother to Oliver Twist, his real name is Edward Leeford, and he continues his mother's villainy in concealing the truth as to Oliver's origins, and in keeping Oliver deprived of the fortune due to him. Monks finds Oliver in Fagin's hands, and pays Fagin to

ensure Oliver is embroiled in crime and liable to conviction. Thanks to Nancy's intervention, Monks is apprehended by Mr Brownlow, who unravels the whole history.

Mowcher, Miss

David Copperfield meets this chirpy, middle-aged dwarf in Yarmouth, when she attends to Steerforth's hair. She becomes the unwitting tool of the treacherous Steerforth by delivering a letter to Emily, and confesses as much to David when she realises the depth of Steerforth's villainy. To her lasting credit, she alone is responsible for the detention of the scurrilous Littimer when he attempts to flee the country in disguise.

Murdstone, Edward

The second husband of Mrs Clara Copperfield in *David Copperfield*. He is amiable to David prior to the marriage, which is so badly handled as to take the boy completely by surprise, but thereafter Murdstone is inflexibly cruel and heartless, both to David and his mother. He arranges for David to go to Salem House school, and, after his mother's death, to work at Murdstone & Grinby in London, and to lodge with the Micawber family. When Miss Trotwood informs him that David has run away to her, he offers to take David back, but is rebuffed.

With a licence from Mr Spenlow, he marries another wealthy young woman, and he and his sister break her spirit, exactly as they had with David's unfortunate mother.

Murdstone, Jane

A passing thought occurred to the adult David Copperfield that "Miss Murdstone, like the pocket instrument called a life preserver, was not so much designed for purposes of protection as of assault". She was a principal oppressor of both David and his mother during the period of his mother's marriage to her brother, Edward Murdstone.

N

Nadgett

The nondescript and secretive enquiry agent in *Martin Chuzzlewit*, employed by Montague Tigg to watch and enquire about Jonas Chuzzlewit in particular. He is also, by strange Dickensian coincidence, Tom Pinch's landlord in London. It is Nadgett who builds the case about Jonas so thoroughly that Tigg has no trouble in bringing Jonas under control. Similarly, Nadgett warns Tigg of Jonas's projected flight to the Continent. Nadgett finally appears with constables to have Jonas arrested for Tigg's murder.

Nancy

The only member of Fagin's gang in *Oliver Twist* with any vestige of conscience and remorse. In a passionate outburst to Fagin, she betrays her revulsion at the intended misuse of Oliver: "I thieved for you when I was a child not half as old as this!" After that, the wily Fagin is guarded about Nancy, and sets Noah Claypole to shadow her. Her betrayal of Monks to Rose Maylie and Mr Brownlow is interpreted by Fagin to Sikes as betrayal of the entire gang, and the unstable Sikes clubs her to death – a scene of shocking and melodramatic violence that Dickens often used in his public readings from his works.

RIGHT: Sally Ann Howes as Kate Nickleby in 1947.
BELOW: Shani Wallis as the ill-fated Nancy in the 1969 musical, *Oliver!*

ABOVE RIGHT: Cedric Hardwick as the money-grabbing Ralph Nickleby, 1947. RIGHT: Mary Merrall played the scatterbrained Mrs Nickleby in the same year.

Nell, Little – See **Trent**

Nickleby, Kate
In *Nicholas Nickleby*, Kate barely manages to rise slightly above the level of Dickens's usual run of heroines, namely pretty, weak and insipid, although she does rebuff the lecherous Sir Mulberry Hawk. Following the changes in Nicholas's fortunes, she marries Frank Cheeryble.

Nickleby, Mrs
Mother of Nicholas Nickleby and Kate, she dotes on her children, but is such a scatterbrain that her stream-of-consciousness style of conversation contributes virtually nothing to any of the discussions. She is a wonderfully comic character, well above the level of the other comic reliefs in the story, and is reputed to have been based, in part at least, on Dickens' own mother, Mrs John Dickens.

Nickleby, Nicholas
The many adventures which befall Nicholas are the basis of the book, a rambling miscellany bursting with characters, and not best organised. Nicholas, his mother and sister Kate, are in an impoverished state, and their appeal for assistance to Nicholas's uncle Ralph receives a poor response. Kate is placed in a dressmaking establishment, while Nicholas is removed to Yorkshire, and the dreadful Squeers school at Dotheboys

Hall. His unhappy experiences there culminate in him thrashing Squeers, before leaving with the unfortunate Smike.

After a short spell trying to teach the Kenwigs children, he joins up with the Vincent Crummles travelling theatre company, in which he has considerable success, but he has to return to London following news of the plight of his sister. His eventual acceptance by the Cheeryble brothers enables him to frustrate his uncle's plans concerning Madeline Bray, whom Nicholas marries. The upright, manly and incorruptible Nicholas wins through against all difficulties, and for much of the time seems far too good to be true.

Nickleby, Ralph

The avaricious, money-lending uncle of Nicholas Nickleby, who does all he can to

hinder rather than help his nephew and niece. He puts Nicholas out of the way with Squeers at Dotheboys Hall, and Kate into a dressmaker's. Later he tries to use her as bait to lure one of his titled clients further into debt. This is frustrated by the return of Nicholas, thus increasing Ralph's hatred of the young

Roger Rees as Nicholas Nickleby in the 1980 stage version.

man, who now has as his companion the hapless Smike, later to be revealed as Ralph's natural son, long believed dead. In time, all his wicked plans rebound on himself, and he taking his own life.

Nipper, Susan

The black-eyed maid in *Dombey and Son*, who is ferociously protective of her charge – young Florence. Despite her fiery manner, she is a most caring servant, and boldly reproves Dombey for

Susan Nipper from *Dombey and Son*, drawn by Phiz, 1842.

his treatment of his daughter, which costs her her job. Toots finds her and brings her back to look after Florence when she has fled from the Dombey home, and after Walter and Florence go overseas, she marries Toots.

Noggs, Newman

Clerk to Ralph Nickleby in *Nicholas Nickleby*. He is a former gentleman who has come down in the world; he is well aware of the devious activities of his unscrupulous employer, and does all he can to expose them. He is the first friend to offer help to Nicholas, and during Nicholas' absence in Yorkshire and elsewhere he manages to keep an eye on Kate's situation. He alerts Nicholas to her predicament, and assists in the downfall of Squeers and Ralph.

Nubbles, Kit

Throughout *The Old Curiosity Shop*, Kit is made blameworthy. He is falsely blamed by Quilp, and thus by Grandfather Trent, for revealing the latter's card gambling. He is rightly blamed by Quilp for calling him "an uglier dwarf than could be seen anywhere

for a penny", and he is blamed by Sampson Brass for the theft of a banknote. In between, Kit's adventures form a secondary theme of the book, for after his discharge from the shop he is hired by the Garlands, loaned to the single gentleman, trapped by Sampson Brass on a trumped-up charge, tried, sentenced to transportation, and saved just in time. His affection for Little Nell remains strong, but after her death he marries Barbara, the Garlands' maid.

ABOVE: Bernard Miles (standing) as Newman Noggs in the 1947 version of *Nicholas Nickleby*.
LEFT: Peter Penrose as Kit Nubbles, 1935.
RIGHT: The rent collector, Mr Pancks, played by Roshan Seth, *Little Dorrit*, 1987.

Nubbles, Mrs

She is a widow, just managing, as a laundress, to keep herself, little Jacob and the baby, when her big son Kit loses his job at the Old Curiosity Shop. He is later given a position with the Garland family, which revives the family fortunes, and on the first quarter day Kit treats his mother and the family to a visit to Astley's Theatre and a feast of oysters. Kit's incarceration is Mrs Nubbles' greatest distress, and his release her most tremendous joy. When Kit marries Barbara, Mrs Nubbles and Barbara's mother take up their abode together.

O

Orlick, Dolge

The strong, rough journeyman-blacksmith employed by Joe Gargery in *Great Expectations*. He harbours enormous resentment against Pip, attacks Mrs Joe, lusts after Biddy, and very nearly succeeds in killing Pip. His burglary of Pumblechook's premises lands him in prison.

P

Pancks, Mr
Employed by Mr Casby as a rent collector in *Little Dorrit*. He involves himself in

research into the Dorrit family, and pops up everywhere in doing so. He succeeds in solving the puzzle of the Dorrit inheritance, which unlocks great riches for the family, and he is generally helpful

to Arthur Clennam. Pancks becomes exasperated with Casby, and humiliates him in front of the residents of Bleeding Heart Yard. He ends up as chief clerk to Doyce & Clennam.

Pecksniff, Charity

The shrewish elder daughter of Seth Pecksniff in *Martin Chuzzlewit*. She is devastated when Jonas marries her sister and not her, and goes to live at Mrs Todgers' boarding house when she realises her father's intention is to woo and marry Mary Graham. Charity is all set to marry Augustus Moddle, one of Mrs Todgers' gentlemen, when she receives on her wedding day a letter from him calling it off.

LEFT: Julie Sawalha as Mercy Pecksniff.
BELOW: "The meekness of Mr Pecksniff and his charming daughters".

Pecksniff, Mercy

The younger daughter of Seth Pecksniff in *Martin Chuzzlewit*. She is a giddy and carefree girl who marries Jonas Chuzzlewit, and immediately lives to regret it, for he treats her cruelly. She resorts to Mrs Todgers from time to time as a relief from her oppression, and behaves very kindly towards old Chuffey, who perceives her predicament. When Jonas dies, old Martin undertakes to care for her.

Pecksniff, Seth

A principal and unifying character in the novel *Martin Chuzzlewit*, supposedly an architect living in the country near Salisbury. Supposedly, because he does nothing in that line himself, relying instead on the work of his various pupils, which he appropriates and passes off as his own. A man of almost unbelievable

insincerity, he manages to delude for a long time the loyal and naïve Tom Pinch, and for a short time the aged and apparently ailing Martin Chuzzlewit, on whose fortune he has decided designs. Not so the younger Martin, who indulges in a violent denunciation of the hyprocrite and his ways when he is summarily dismissed by Pecksniff at old Martin's request.

The old man declares to Pecksniff: "[Some] will say . . . that you have lied, and fawned, and wormed yourself through dirty ways into my favour; by such concessions and such crooked deeds, such meanness and vile endurances, as nothing could repay". Pecksniff little realises that this accurate forecast marks the beginning of his sincerity being put to the test by old Martin, who needs to see how far the over-confident Pecksniff will go in his calumny and deceit. Pecksniff succumbs to Jonas when entreated to invest in Tigg's spurious company, and at the end is not only denounced by old Martin, but is ruined financially.

Peggotty, Clara

Loving nurse to David Copperfield, and companion to his widowed mother. She is seriously concerned at the harsh treatment of them both by Murdstone and his sister, but is helpless to intervene, and when the mother's funeral is over she is discharged. She returns to Yarmouth, and marries the miserly carrier Barkis. David sees her occasionally when he stays with her brother Daniel and family in the boat house. After Barkis dies, she is quite reasonably provided for and is always ready to help David, and even his aunt, who gradually softens towards her, and they settle down together.

Peggotty, Daniel

Brother of David Copperfield's affectionate nurse Clara. He lives with various family members in his boat house at Yarmouth, and is grief-stricken when his beloved niece Emily runs off with the heartless Steerforth after being betrothed to Ham, Daniel's nephew. Daniel

dedicates himself to searching for Emily, and eventually finds her with the help of the disgraced Martha. A rough-and-ready seaman with a heart of gold, he takes both girls to Australia, along with Mrs Gummidge, and years later returns to report on their prosperity.

Peggotty, Ham

The nephew of Daniel Peggotty in *David Copperfield*. He is a big, simple, lumbering boatbuilder who becomes betrothed to Little Emily on the evening that David and Steerforth visit the boat home at Yarmouth. The consquence of that visit is Emily's elopement with the unscrupulous Steerforth: a devastating blow to Ham. When Steerforth has deserted Emily abroad, and sets off to return to England, his vessel is wrecked in a storm off Yarmouth, and Ham attempts to rescue some of the survivors. Both he and Steerforth are drowned.

Pegler, Mrs

The mysterious old lady in *Hard Times* who periodically travels a long way to Coketown, just to get a glimpse of the great Bounderby, so she tells Stephen Blackpool. After the bank robbery she is suspected of being involved, and is seized by Mrs Sparsit on her next visit. She turns out to be Bounderby's mother, banished to a great distance and directed to keep her relationship secret, so that he can perpetrate the myth of a cruel, hard, impoverished childhood and youth. Her disclosure of the truth pricks the bubble of his trumpeted humility.

Perker, Mr

The snuff-taking lawyer of Gray's Inn, in *The Pickwick Papers*, is first introduced as Mr Wardle's attorney, during the pursuit of the eloping Jingle and Rachael Wardle. He re-appears at the Eatanswill election as agent for Samuel Slumkey, the victorious candidate, and later still in his most important role as Mr Pickwick's dutiful lawyer arranging the defence in the case of Bardell versus Pickwick, and in the eventual release of Pickwick from the Fleet Prison. His attempts to restrain his excitable client from venting his righteous indignation on Dodson and Fogg meet with little success.

LEFT: Michael Redgrave as Peggotty, *David Copperfield*, 1969.
BELOW: Peggotty drawn by Fred Barnard.

Petowker, Henrietta

"Of the Theatre Royal, Drury Lane", in *Nicholas Nickleby*. The association with a celebrated London theatre always provided valuable advertising copy, as Vincent Crummles was quick to point out. Miss Petowker, an old friend of Mrs Crummles, joined the company for a short engagement, as a means of marrying Mr Lillyvick away from his rapacious relations, the Kenwigs, where Nicholas had met her earlier. Later, Henrietta ran off with a half-pay captain.

Pickwick, Samuel

Although the central character in *The Pickwick Papers*, Mr Pickwick is frequently a passive figure, against whom the other protagonists operate. With an extraordinary childlike innocence, he makes his way through the adventures of the quartet from the Pickwick Club in such a state of unworldly naivety that one wonders how he succeeded in business to amass the wealth he is clearly able to rely upon for his benevolence.

Pickwick is often taken in by poseurs and charlatans, and is at his most incompetent when dealing with women, with the possible exception of old Mrs Wardle, towards whom he displays admirable tact and gallantry. Faced with anyone younger, like Mrs Bardell, Miss Witherfield or Miss Tompkins, he becomes a dithering jelly of indecision and helplessness.

The most surprising thing about *The Pickwick Papers*, Dickens's least planned and plotted book (it can hardly be called a

"Mr Pinch is amazed by an unexpected apparition", an illustration by Phiz from *Martin Chuzzlewit*.

novel), is that, despite its improvisation, in the urgent climate of writing for monthly instalments, it is still so good. Of course there are faults, more probably than in any other Dickens book, but these are largely due to Dickens rapidly learning his craft, and they are readily overlooked as the reader is carried along in the almost headlong romp of the Pickwickians through the various episodes of their adventures.

The abiding impression left by the book is the lasting relationship between Mr Pickwick and Sam Weller. For Pickwick, Sam becomes a surrogate son, and for Sam, the figure of Pickwick becomes a substitute for the father he probably seldom saw, since Tony Weller must have been away driving long-distance coaches for much of Sam's upbringing. The re-appearance of the two of them in *Master Humphrey's Clock* is a great disappointment.

Mr Pickwick visits the lawyers, Dodson and Fogg.

Pinch, Ruth

Sister of Tom in *Martin Chuzzlewit*, and an example of how far-reaching the blighting effect of Pecksniffery could be. While working in London as a governess, she is visited with a message by the condescending Pecksniffs, and as a consequence she falls into disfavour with her employer. When Tom calls on her he defends her vigorously against unjust criticism, and takes her away with him. She keeps house for him, and later marries John Westlock.

Pinch, Tom

In *Martin Chuzzlewit* Pinch is the unbelievably loyal general dogsbody to the odious Pecksniff, in whom Pinch can see no wrong, and whom he defends against all criticism. Pinch's blindness to

Pecksniff's hypocrisy is baffling, especially since Pinch himself is not without talents. He is "one of those strange creatures who never decline into an ancient appearance, but look their oldest when they are very young, and get it over at once". He becomes enamoured of old Martin's companion, Mary Graham, and only when she discloses to him the overtures that Pecksniff has made to her does Pinch realise how long he has been deceived by his employer.

When Pecksniff discharges him in front of old Martin, it is Pinch's loyalty to young Martin that prevents him from exposing Pecksniff's machinations, just as Pecksniff had anticipated. Pinch departs to London, where an unknown benefactor provides him with a job, and he is able to accommodate his loving sister. Pinch is such a mainstay of the story, it is as well he is so likeable.

Pip

Real name Philip Pirrip, he is the hero of *Great Expectations*. He is an orphan, and is "brought up by hand" by his ferocious sister, who is married to Joe Gargery. At Miss Havisham's he meets Estella, and forms a keen and urgent desire to become a gentleman, but he is apprenticed to Joe as a blacksmith instead.

Pip is the central figure of this compact and finely executed novel, and learns that he has great expectations, which he mistakenly believes originate from Miss Havisham. His good fortune is dealt to him through the hand of the lawyer Jaggers, and he selfishly turns his back on his former friends, by whom he is now embarrassed. He is shocked and humbled when he learns that his benefactor is really Magwitch, a convict he once helped on the marshes, who was transported to Australia, made a fortune, and has now unwisely returned in secret to see his protegé. Magwitch is recaptured, and dies, leaving Pip ill and in debt. He receives help from Herbert Pocket, whom

George Breakston as Pip in *Great Expectations* from 1934.

he had once covertly assisted, and finally meets up again with a chastened Estella on the site of Miss Havisham's home, Satis House.

Pipchin, Mrs

Ogress and child-queller of Brighton in *Dombey and Son*, to whose school little Paul is sent. While the pupils' meals are "of the farinaceous and vegetable kind", Mrs Pipchin has mutton chops, and Paul, in his direct way, points out the unfairness. She is later engaged as housekeeper at the Dombey home in London. Her character was drawn from Mrs Roylance, the woman to whom Dickens was consigned in his dreadful days at the blacking factory.

Herbert Pocket from *Great Expectations*, as played by Alec Guinness in 1946.

Plornish, Thomas

Out-of-work plasterer of Bleeding Heart Yard, and a good friend to Little Dorrit, Clennam uses Plornish to pay off Tip's debt. William Dorrit sets him up in a little business – one of the few good things arising from the Dorrit fortune – and the Plornishes try to help Clennam when he is in prison.

Pocket, Herbert

Pip's close friend and companion in *Great Expectations*. A thoroughly likeable, frank, straightforward young man, he has "a natural incapacity to do anything secret and mean". Pip covertly helps Herbert by financing a position for him with a shipping merchant. Herbert, in turn, helps Pip in hiding Magwitch, alias Provis, and in the vain effort to get him out of the country. When Pip's good

fortune disappears on the death of Magwitch, Herbert provides Pip with a clerkship.

Pocket, Matthew
Father of Herbert, and cousin to Miss Havisham, in *Great Expectations*. A gentle, scholarly man, he has the misfortune of being married to a totally incapable and incurably snobbish wife, whose inability to cope with their large family causes him virtually to pull his own hair out. Pip goes to him for cultural instruction, and later intercedes with Miss Havisham to leave Matthew a handsome bequest.

Price, Matilda
One-time friend of Fanny Squeers, in *Nicholas Nickleby*. She is betrothed to, and marries, John Browdie, to the extreme jealousy of Fanny, who is unable to find a husband. 'Tilda mischievously encourages Fanny in the belief that she has a strong chance with the young, handsome Nicholas, but her efforts only end in dispute. Later, as Mrs Browdie, 'Tilda proves a good friend to Nicholas and Smike, and helps many of the boys at the break-up of Dotheboys Hall.

Pross, Miss
A lesser battleaxe of the Betsey Trotwood category in *A Tale of Two Cities*. Impoverished by her scoundrel of a brother, Solomon, she has become the companion of Lucie Manette, and grumbles when "hundreds of people" (i.e., Darnay and Carton) come to visit her. She softens a little towards Jarvis Lorry when she realises that he too is concerned with the welfare of the family, and shows her true mettle when confronted by Mme Defarge.

Pumblechook, Uncle
Joe Gargery's uncle in *Great Expectations*. A seed and corn merchant in the nearest town to the forge, he is "a large, hard-breathing, middle-aged, slow man, with a mouth like a fish, dull staring eyes, and sandy hair standing upright on his head". Pip cannot stand the pompous hyprocrite, who invariably seeks to take credit for the progress Pip has made. He is the channel through which Pip is first summoned to Miss Havisham's, a dubious benefit in the light of all the subsequent unhappiness.

Robert Morley played Uncle Pumblechook in *Great Expectations*, 1975.

Q

Quilp, Betsy

The persecuted wife of Daniel Quilp, in
The Old Curiosity Shop. In Quilp's eyes
she can do nothing right, but her time
comes when the evil dwarf drowns
without leaving a will, and she inherits all
his property. She is remarried to a smart
young fellow, and they lead "a merry life
upon the dead dwarf's money".

Quilp, Daniel

The evil money-lender in *The Old
Curiosity Shop*. The personification of
wickedness, Quilp is probably the most
repulsive of all Dickens's grotesque
characters, with no redeeming features.
The energy he expends in venting his
spite with physical and mental cruelty
knows no bounds. He lends money to
Grandfather Trent in the mistaken belief
that there is great hidden wealth, and
when Trent and Nell flee from the shop,
which Quilp has seized against the debt,
his pursuit drives them further and
further afield. He terrorises his fearful
little wife, and intimidates the toadying
Sampson Brass, whose best client he is.
When his misdeeds finally become
known, he is pursued by the police, and
drowns at his own wharf.

R

Rachael

The factory worker who loves Stephen
Blackpool in *Hard Times*, and knows
nothing can come of their relationship,
since he is still shackled to his violent,
drunken wife. She is distraught when he
is accused of robbery, and tries in vain to
clear his name. Sissy and Rachael
accidentally find the mineshaft into which
Stephen has fallen, and try, in vain, to
save him.

LEFT: Hay Petrie playing Daniel Quilp in
The Old Curiosity Shop, 1935.
RIGHT: An illustration depicting Rogue
Riderhood from *Our Mutual Friend*.

Riderhood, Rogue

One-time waterside partner of Gaffer
Hexam in *Our Mutual Friend*, he
denounces Hexam for a murder, in the
hope of a big reward. He is a shiftless,
dishonest rogue, forever talking about his
honest day's work by the sweat of his
brow – of which he has no experience. He
eventually secures a job as a lock-keeper,
and becomes aware of Bradley
Headstone's interest in Wrayburn's
activities. He also notices Headstone's
imitation of his own attire, and rightly
concludes that Headstone plans to
implicate him in some crime.

When the Wrayburn murder (as is first
thought) is discovered, he follows
Headstone, and retrieves the
incriminating clothes Headstone discards.
He then tries to blackmail Headstone,
and in their final confrontation both are
killed.

Rigaud

The first character to appear in *Little Dorrit*, he is introduced in a Marseilles prison cell. Tried for the murder of his wife, he is acquitted, and public anger at his release forces him to adopt the name of Lagnier. He turns up at various points in the story, particularly at the Clennam premises under the name of Blandois, where he seeks to blackmail Mrs Clennam with documents that Flintwinch has stolen from the Clennam house. At the time of the collapse of the house, he is in the building, and is killed.

Rudge, Barnaby

Although the title character of the book, Barnaby Rudge is not the sole point of focus through the story, as the adventures of a number of other characters have

Barnaby Rudge's encounter with the raven Grip.

similar prominence. He is a half-witted, but relatively harmless, young man, extremely interested in animals and wild life; his constant companion is Grip, a raven. With his mother, he leaves their home and heads for London, where he becomes unwittingly involved in the Gordon Riots, and encounters his father in Newgate Prison. He is only saved from execution by the intervention of Gabriel Varden. Barnaby and his mother return to Chigwell, and settle down on the Maypole farm, where he is happy among the animals.

The novel is one of the less popular of Dickens' books (as well as one of the most violent), and was his first venture into an historical period far removed from his own. The scope of the plot goes far beyond what Dickens had hitherto attempted, and the sweep of the action of the Gordon Riots is vividly handled.

Rudge, Mr

The father of Barnaby Rudge, and steward to Reuben Haredale, the father of Emma. When Reuben is found dead and Rudge missing, the latter is believed to be dead also, but he re-appears and tries to blackmail his wife, who keeps trying to flee from him. He is finally apprehended by Geoffrey Haredale, Reuben's brother, at the height of the Gordon Riots, and finds himself in a cell in Newgate with his own son.

Rudge, Mrs

The compassionate mother of Barnaby Rudge, who strives to keep her beloved simpleton of a son out of the reach of his murderous father, who is believed dead by all but Mrs Rudge. To achieve this she takes Barnaby to London, but they are still pursued. Despite her impassioned objections, Barnaby is enrolled with the Gordon Rioters, and lands in jail. When she visits him, she reveals his father's misdeeds. She also sees her husband, who shows no remorse. Barnaby is saved from execution at the last minute, and afterwards, she lives with him on the Maypole farm.

S

Sally, Old

An inmate of the parish workhouse in *Oliver Twist* who nurses Oliver's mother through childbirth and death. On her own deathbed she confesses to Mrs Corney that she had stolen something gold from the dead girl. The pawn ticket in Sally's dead hand produces Agnes' locket and ring.

Sapsea, Thomas

Pompous old fool of an auctioneer in *Edwin Drood*, who becomes Mayor of Cloisterham. He is so full of self-importance he is unable to grasp scarcely anything of what is going on, and immediately assumes Neville's guilt. Said to be based on Jesse Thomas, Mayor of Rochester in 1857, and an auctioneer.

Scadder, Zephaniah

The crooked land agent who sells Martin Chuzzlewit 50 acres of worthless land in "Eden", thereby ruining his prospects of advancement in America, and almost causing his death from fever.

Scott, Tom

Quilp's extraordinary errand-boy in *The Old Curiosity Shop*. Tom was forever standing on his head or walking on his hands, unless avoiding missiles hurled at him by his vicious master. Curiously, Tom was the only person to appear upset over Quilp's demise, but he soon got over it, and fittingly became a successful tumbler.

Scrooge, Ebenezer

Almost certainly the best-known name of any Dickens character, and a name that has become a part of the English language. In *A Christmas Carol* Dickens re-works an idea that began as an interlude in *The Pickwick Papers*, where Gabriel Grub, the sexton, is transformed by spirits from an old curmudgeon into a reasonably benevolent soul, Grub being a plainly recognisable prototype of Ebenezer.

Scrooge appears on Christmas Eve as a "squeezing, wrenching, grasping, scraping, clutching, covetous old sinner . . . He carried his own low temperature always about with him". He rebuffs his nephew Fred, when invited to spend Christmas with him, with the now-famous response "Bah! Humbug". He very grudgingly agrees that his clerk Cratchit can have Christmas Day off, and heads home, where he encounters the various ghosts that take him to scenes which affect him deeply, and bring about increasing remorse. When he finds

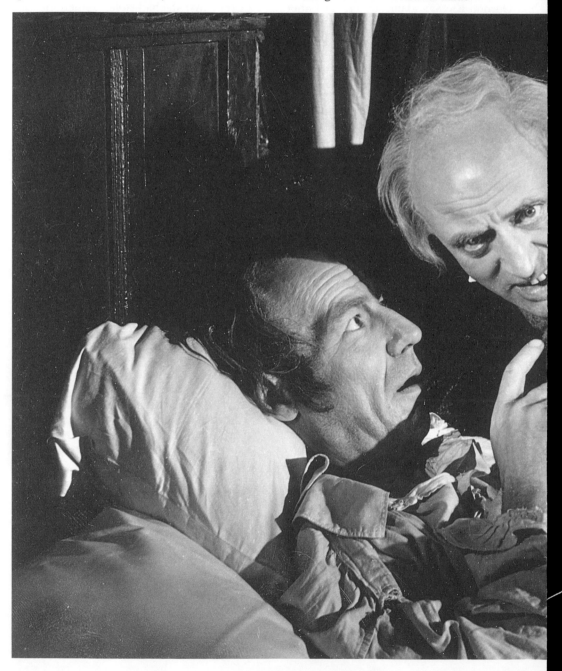

himself again in his own bedchamber, he hastens to make amends for all his previous defaulting. The story, in so many different forms, has become one of the most celebrated in all world literature, even among many who have never read it.

Alastair Sim as the miser Scrooge listens to his partner Jacob Marley (in bed) in the 1951 film, *Scrooge*.

Short, Trotters

Real name Harris, in *The Old Curiosity Shop*, but known as Short because of his size. He is the affable partner in Codlin's Punch and Judy show, and more kindly towards Nell and her grandfather, who accompany Codlin and Short during part of their travels.

Sikes, Bill

The ruffianly burglar in *Oliver Twist* is an unpredictably violent character of whom the entire Fagin gang is afraid. One of the most celebrated burglars in literature, he is steadfastly served by Nancy, who remains utterly loyal to him throughout. He little understands the scheming subtleties of Fagin's mind, but eventually grasps Fagin's allusions to betrayal, and, as Fagin expected and probably intended, rushes off and commits the most brutal murder of Nancy, whose devotion to him is unshakeable, even in her last moments. The awfulness of the crime turns the remainder of the gang against him, and

ABOVE: James Harcourt as The Single Gentleman, Dick Tubb as Codlin and Roddy Hughes as Short, 1935.

although he flees, he is cornered by an enraged mob and accidentally falls and hangs himself.

Single Gentleman, The

Brother to Little Nell's grandfather in *The Old Curiosity Shop*. Supposedly Master Humphrey, who narrates the first few chapters of the story, which began in the fourth part of *Master Humphrey's Clock* a weekly miscellany founded by Dickens in 1840. The single gentleman, shrewd and beneficent, lodges at Brass's premises, hoping to trace his brother and Nell, and pursues them as vigorously as Quilp, but with different intentions. He is the link with the Garlands, and assists with the exoneration of Kit, the resuscitation of Swiveller, the punishment of Brass, and the location of Nell in her final resting place.

BELOW LEFT: Robert Newton as Bill Sikes in *Oliver Twist*, 1948.
BELOW: Sikes and his faithful dog as drawn by Fred Barnard.

Skewton, The Hon Mrs

The false, vain and affected mother of Edith Granger in *Dombey and Son*. "Her age, which is about seventy, and her dress, which would have been youthful for twenty-seven", she has been around the circuit of spas and resorts for years, seeking to marry off her daughter. When the catch of Dombey is made, she believes that they are both well settled for life, but misjudges her indomitable daughter, and the break-up of the unhappy marriage causes her to have a stroke.

Skimpole, Harold

This smarmy sponger is tolerated at Bleak House by Jarndyce, who considers him a perfect child. He is, in fact, selfish and unprincipled, and sells Jo to Inspector Bucket for a five pound note. Jarndyce eventually cools towards Skimpole because of this, and because of his continued sponging on the impecunious Richard Carstone, despite Jarndyce's requests to him to desist.

Dickens wrote to his friend Leigh Hunt, apologising for incorporating too closely many of Hunt's characteristics in the person of Skimpole, but adjuring him: "Separate in your own mind what you see of yourself from what other people tell you that they see".

Slackbridge

In *Hard Times*, the rabble-rousing trade-union delegate who persuades the Coketown millworkers to shun Stephen Blackpool because, for genuine personal reasons, he will not join in their United Aggregate Tribunal. Slackbridge is totally unconcerned that this action will cost Stephen his livelihood. Dickens paints a harsh portrait of a man whom he describes as an agitator.

Slammer, Doctor

The fiery surgeon of the 97th Regiment in *The Pickwick Papers*. Slammer feels himself affronted by Jingle at the Charity Ball in Rochester, when the wealthy widow Mrs Budger is considerably taken with the manners and behaviour of the younger man, to Slammer's enormous discomfiture. The subsequent confrontation nearly results in a duel between Slammer and Winkle, whose coat Jingle had been wearing.

LEFT: Mrs Skewton, drawn by Phiz, 1842.
BELOW Harold Skimpole (centre), illustrated by Phiz for *Bleak House*.

Sleary, Mr

The genial circus proprietor in *Hard Times*, who exhorts Gradgrind to "make the best of us: not the worst", for people must be amused. This philosophy is repeated to Gradgrind at the end of the story, when he is better able to appreciate it. Sleary agrees to Sissy Jupe going to the Gradgrind home, and is later instrumental in ensuring young Tom's escape abroad, using his trained horse, dog, and circus friends to foil Bitzer's intervention.

Sliderskew, Peg

The grouchy old servant of the miserly Arthur Gride, in *Nicholas Nickleby*. She strongly resents Gride's intended marriage to Madeline Bray, which will displace her, and in revenge she steals a box of documents which just happens to contain a will bequeathing a great deal of valuable property to Madeline. The attempt by Squeers to retrieve it for the devious Ralph Nickleby ends with both the unspeakable Squeers and Peg Sliderskew in custody.

Harry Markham as Mr Sleary, the genial circus owner in *Hard Times*, a 1977 production.
The Smallweed family as illustrated by Phiz for *Bleak House*.

Smallweed, Grandfather

The little chairbound money-lender and bill-discounter in *Bleak House*, and a brother-in-law of Krook. He is a nasty-tempered old skinflint in league with Tulkinghorn, to whom he delivers Lady Dedlock's letters to her lover. When Tulkinghorn is killed, he seeks money from Sir Leicester for them.

Smike

Discovered by Nicholas Nickleby at Dotheboys Hall, the pathetic Smike is cruelly treated by the Squeers family. Nicholas prevents Squeers from flogging Smike, and leaves the school is disgust; Smike begs to accompany him. Their happy sojourn in the Crummles theatre company is ended by an urgent message from Newman Noggs. Back in London, Smike is briefly and terrifyingly recaptured by Squeers, but is released by John Browdie. Ralph Nickleby and Squeers falsely claim that Smike is Snawley's son, but Smike stays with Nicholas, and it transpires that the poor, ailing lad is really Ralph's own son, long

believed dead. Smike dies in peaceful
seclusion, having confessed to Nicholas
his love for Kate.

Snawley, Mr

Early in the story of *Nicholas Nickleby*,
Snawley is seen depositing his two
stepsons with Squeers, well knowing their
unhappy fate at his hands. Snawley is
later recruited by Ralph Nickleby to
produce false evidence that he is the
father of Smike. When this fails, and
trouble looms, Snawley betrays the
conspirators, Ralph and Squeers.

Snevellicci, Miss

A leading lady in the Crummles theatrical
company in *Nicholas Nickleby*, "who
could do anything from a medley dance to
Lady Macbeth". She is very attracted to
the well-bred Nicholas, but in vain.

Snodgrass, Augustus

The poetic Pickwickian in *The Pickwick
Papers*. Other than a dreamy disposition,
artistic apparel and a stated "strong

BELOW: Snodgrass, as portrayed by Lionel
Murton in *The Pickwick Papers*, 1952.
RIGHT: Aubrey Woods (Smike) and Derek
Bond (Nicholas Nickleby) in the 1947 film.

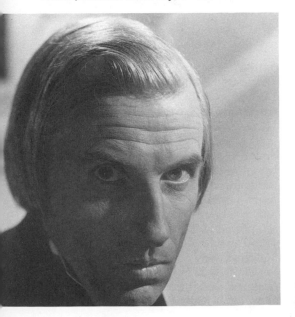

poetic turn", there is no real evidence of Snodgrass' poetry. He remains more in the background of the Pickwickian quartet until near the end of the book, when his attachment to Emily Wardle, with whom he has been in communication since the preceding Christmas, becomes known to her father and Mr Pickwick. "Very bad spectacles we must have worn not to have discovered it before", comments Wardle. When married to Emily, Snodgrass settles at a small farm at Dingley Dell, where his mysterious reputation as a great poet follows him.

Snubbin, Serjeant

Counsel for Mr Pickwick in the breach-of-promise case brought by Mrs Bardell. Arrogant and abstracted when interviewed by Mr Pickwick, he proves to be totally ineffectual when he appears in court. Described by Mr Perker as being at the very top of his profession, he is no match for the brow-beating Buzfuz.

Sowerberry, Mr

The undertaker who relieves the workhouse of Oliver Twist for five pounds. He seeks to use the melancholy Oliver as a mute in funeral processions, but the project is short-lived. Sowerberry is reasonably kind to the boy, but the fracas involving Noah Claypole and Mrs Sowerberry obliges him to thrash Oliver, who then runs away.

Sowerberry, Mrs

Wife of the undertaker in *Oliver Twist*. She is an early member of Dickens' brigade of unreasonable, unrestrainable women, who disrupt their husbands' lives and activities by their illogical and volatile behaviour.

Sparkler, Edmund

The son of Mrs Merdle's first marriage in *Little Dorrit*. He is a foolish young idler, who cannot keep away from the fickle and fractious Fanny Dorrit. Her advent into Society enables him to marry her, and they survive because their connection

with the Barnacles finds him a prime position in the Circumlocution Office.

Sparsit, Mrs

The venomous aristocratic widow who acts as Bounderby's housekeeper in *Hard Times*. As a counterpoint to his tiresome boasting about his own lowly origins, Bounderby is forever lauding Mrs Sparsit and her background to the skies. This leads her to think that she might one day become Mrs Bounderby. Very put out by his marriage to Louisa, she tries to discredit Louisa after observing Harthouse's meeting with her, but only succeeds in exposing Bounderby's mother, and the truth about his upbringing. Bounderby thus dispenses with her services.

Spenlow, Dora

David Copperfield, always susceptible to pretty young females, falls in love at first sight with the daughter of his principal. The unworldly David is long unable to discern how spoilt and empty-headed Dora is, and she never develops beyond being a helpless baby-doll figure. This is

Pamela Franklin as Dora Spenlow in the 1969 *David Copperfield*.

Susannah York (Mrs Cratchit), Edward Woodward (Christmas Present) and George C Scott (Scrooge), 1984.

even recognised by Betsey Trotwood, who calls her "Little Blossom". They are not married very long before she dies.

Spirits of Christmas

These appear in *A Christmas Carol*, variously referred to by Dickens as spirits or ghosts. Scrooge is warned by the ghost of his former partner, Jacob Marley, that he will be haunted by these spirits. The first, of Christmas Past, takes Scrooge back through episodes of his own past. The second, of Christmas Present, shows him jolly Christmas preparations, and a moving and revealing view of the interior of the Cratchits' home, where Scrooge learns that he is the ogre of the family. As well as less fortunate gatherings, he also sees how genuine his nephew Fred is, and receives a reminder of the perpetual presence of ignorance and want. The third Spirit, that of Christmas Yet To Come, shows circumstances of death, but does not reveal to Scrooge whether they are "the shadows of things that will be, or . . . things that may be, only".

Squeers, Fanny

At one time a friend of Matilda Price, Fanny is attracted to Nicholas Nickleby, who spurns her advances. She reports the beating of her father by Nicholas in a priceless letter to Ralph: "My pa requests me to write to you, the doctors considering it doubtful whether he will ever recuvver the use of his legs which prevents his holding a pen". When Matilda Price marries the farmer, John Browdie, Fanny is further put out, and their later acrimonious encounter in London leads to Browdie releasing Smike after his recapture by Squeers.

Squeers, Master Wackford

In *Nicholas Nickleby* the young Wackford is used by his father as a deceitful advertisement for the well-being of the boys in his care. Squeers delights in seeing his detestable son feed his plump frame at other people's expense, and clothe himself in garments sent for the other boys, whom he enjoys kicking and pinching at every opportunity. He recognises Smike in London, and assists in his recapture.

Squeers, Mrs

"If the young man [Nicholas Nickleby] comes to be a teacher here, let him understand, at once, that we don't want any foolery about the boys". snaps Mrs Squeers. "They have the brimstone and treacle, partly because if they hadn't something or other in the way of medicine they'd be always ailing . . . and partly because it spoils their appetites and comes cheaper than breakfast and dinner". The administration of this compound is the familiar and lasting image of Mrs Squeers, who is a well-matched accomplice of her husband in the ill-treatment of the boys.

LEFT: Dame Sybil Thorndike as the evil Mrs Squeers in a film of *Nicholas Nickleby*.
RIGHT: Wackford Squeers, as played by Alfred Dayton in 1947, the villainous overseer of Dotheboys Hall.

Squeers, Wackford

"He had but one eye and the popular prejudice runs in favour of two." The cruel schoolmaster in *Nicholas Nickleby* whose establishment in Yorkshire was typical of a number of such places in which unwanted children were placed, Squeers is one of Dickens's gloriously villainous creations, and was reputedly based on William Shaw, whose Bowes Academy, near Greta Bridge, was the original of Dotheboys Hall. Dickens' visit to Yorkshire in 1838 led him to expose such premises and practices with his stark depiction of the Squeers family, the school and the ill-treatment of the boys.

When Squeers starts to flog Smike for trying to run away, Nicholas rebels, thrashes Squeers and leaves, taking Smike with him. Squeers recaptures Smike in London, but the timely intervention of John Browdie cancels Squeers' triumph. The further attempt by Squeers and Ralph Nickleby to claim Smike as Snawley's son is no more successful. Squeers' purloining of the Bray will from Peg Sliderskew is forcibly prevented by Noggs and Frank Cheeryble, after which Squeers is transported for seven years.

Steerforth, James

David Copperfield first meets him at
Salem House school, where his arrogance
– born of money and position – is first
exhibited. For years the naïve David is
bedazzled by this smooth, accomplished,
completely conscienceless young man.
Seeing Little Emily just engaged to Ham
and wanting to be a lady, presents
Steerforth with an irresistible challenge,
and he causes enormous pain and
suffering by running off abroad with her
just prior to her intended marriage.
Tiring of her, he leaves her to be married
to his servant Littimer, and pursues a
restless, roving life at sea. Returning to
England, he is drowned in a fierce storm
off Yarmouth.

Steerforth, Mrs

Although touched by the boyish affection
of David Copperfield for her son James,
Mrs Steerforth remains haughtily
condescending to this young man of an
inferior class, and can see no wrong in the
son she has spoiled and indulged all his
life. When he entices Emily away with
him, it is Emily who is held by her to be
to blame for James's actions. Her single-

ABOVE: Steerforth (centre) and Mr Mills
from *David Copperfield*.
RIGHT: Dr Strong reading his dictionary to
Mr Dick, drawn by Barnard for *David
Copperfield*.

mindedness leaves her shattered by the
news of James' death.

Strong, Annie

The beautiful young wife of Doctor
Strong in *David Copperfield*. Her
childhood friend, Jack Maldon, pays her
such close attention that tongues are
bound to wag. The doctor is oblivious,
until Uriah Heep raises the matter for his
own ends, but Annie's innocence is
established, no thanks to her thoughtless
and pushy mother.

Strong, Doctor

Head of the school to which David
Copperfield is sent by his aunt, Strong's
marriage to the very much younger Annie
is the subject of a sub-plot in the novel,
involving Jack Maldon and Annie's
perpetually interfering mother, Mrs
Markleham. The doctor is idolised by the
boys, and devotes most of his time to the

compilation of his new dictionary, which the head boy calculates will take 1,649 years to complete. The doctor continues to trust his wife, until Uriah Heep makes known to him the suspicions of other people as to the intentions of Jack Maldon. Fortunately, David, Mr Dick and Miss Trotwood are on hand to frustrate Heep, and the marriage is happily re-affirmed.

Stryver, Mr

Learned counsel in *A Tale of Two Cities*, "Stout, loud, red, bluff, and free from any drawback of delicacy". Stryver relies heavily on the detailed preparation work of cases done for him by Sydney Carton. With his depiction of Stryver, Dickens makes clear that he still does not think much of lawyers. Having successfully defended Darnay, with Carton's help, Stryver has become friendly with the Manette family. Feeling the need for a wife, he announces that he intends to ask for Lucie's hand, but when Lorry advises him against the plan, he affects indifference to the whole idea.

Dickens acknowledged that Stryver was based on Edwin James, a disbarred barrister, after which one Gordon Allen, another barrister, was found almost starving in James' chambers. Obviously Allen formed the basis for Stryver's "jackal", Sydney Carton.

Summerson, Esther

Heroine and principal unifying character in *Bleak House*. After an oppressed childhood, she finds herself a ward of John Jarndyce, and a chaperone for Ada Clare, also living with Jarndyce. Esther acts as housekeeper at Bleak House, and helps to tend some of the poor families in the nearby brickfields. Following a near-

fatal bout of smallpox, her looks are impaired, but her modest, selfless, spirit of service is undiminished. Lady Dedlock confesses to her that she is her mother, and when Lady Dedlock disappears, Esther accompanies Inspector Bucket in his search for her. Jarndyce understands that while Esther would marry him, as they agreed, she prefers Allan Woodcourt, and he gives them his blessing, along with a new house.

Mr Guppy and Ester Summerson as drawn by Phiz for *Bleak House*.

Swiveller, Dick

The rakish Swiveller is party to a plan to marry Nell for the money believed to be coming to her from her grandfather. Her disappearance from the Old Curiosity Shop frustrates the plan, and Swiveller is taken up by Quilp in the belief that such a plan could still succeed. Quilp gets Sampson Brass to employ Swiveller, who becomes the negotiator with the single gentleman lodging on the first floor, and feeds information as to his activities to Quilp via Brass. When Quilp decides Dick Swiveller's usefulness is over, he

orders Brass to discharge him.
Dick falls very ill and is nursed by the
half-starved drudge, Marchioness. When
he recovers she tells him of the conspiracy
to frame Kit, and this information secures
Kit's release. Dick finally receives an
annuity, puts the illiterate Marchioness
through school, and then marries her.

ABOVE: Dick Swiveller and the lodger from
The Old Curiosity Shop.
BELOW: Jolly Mark Tapley illustrated for an
early edition of *Martin Chuzzlewit.*

T

Tapley, Mark

Charles Dickens himself has been cited as
a possible original for *Chuzzlewit*'s
Tapley, as Dickens endured great
discomforts during his first visit to
America, and was determined to remain
cheerful under all circumstances. Mark
Tapley's desire to thrive under adversity
leads him to quit his job as an ostler at
the Blue Dragon, and to accompany
young Martin to America, where he
anticipates much more adversity to
challenge him. On their return, he
participates in the downfall of Pecksniff,
marries Mrs Lupin, and amends the
name of the inn to the Jolly Tapley.

Tappertit, Simon

Apprentice to the locksmith Gabriel Varden in *Barnaby Rudge*. "An old-fashioned, thin-faced, sleek-haired, sharp-nosed, small-eyed little fellow, very little more than five feet high, and thoroughly convinced in his own mind that he is above middle size; rather tall, in fact, than otherwise". The blind man's assessment of Tappertit as "a conceited, bragging, empty-headed, duck-legged idiot" seems pretty accurate. He is a silly agitator who gets mixed up in the Gordon Riots, during which he loses both his legs – his pride and joy. He sets up as a boot-black, prospers and marries, and his wife controls him by taking away his wooden legs when necessary.

Tartar, Lieutenant

Ex-naval officer in *Edwin Drood*, who occupies adjacent chambers to Neville Landless in Staple Inn, and who facilitates communication between Rosa and Helena. He is an old acquaintance of Crisparkle, and there are signs of mutual attraction with Rosa.

Tattycoram

In *Little Dorrit*. Tattycoram is taken from the Foundling Hospital in London as a maid for Minnie Meagles, and is so named by the Meagles family in place of the institution's label of Harriet Beadle. She is subject to sudden and passionate outbursts of temper against her situation, and lacks any appreciation of the opportunity that has been given her. This intrigues the cold and haughty Miss Wade, who entices her away from the Meagles household, but in the end fails to hold her, and Tattycoram returns to ask forgiveness, bringing with her the stolen Clennam documents.

Tigg, Montague

Initially an associate of Chevy Slyme, who is a distant poor relative of old Martin Chuzzlewit, Tigg is a cadger and a small-time con man, dunning young Martin for a half-crown at the pawnbroker's. In a remarkable transformation, he turns himself into Tigg Montague, chairman of the lavishly appointed, and utterly crooked Anglo Bengalee Disinterested Loan and Life Assurance Company. Learning of Jonas Chuzzlewit's scheme to kill off Anthony, Tigg forces Jonas to invest heavily in the company, and also to get Pecksniff to do so. Tigg employs Nadgett to watch Jonas, and Nadgett is able to expose Jonas as Tigg's murderer. Tigg's one saving grace seems to be his concern for the welfare of young Bailey.

Tim, Tiny – see *Cratchit*

Todgers, Mrs

Landlady of a boarding house in *Martin Chuzzlewit*, to which Pecksniff resorts when in London. Although it is for men only, she accedes to Pecksniff's request that his daughters may stay there; the gentlemen regulars are overcome. Mrs Todgers has had romantic hopes of Pecksniff, but when Charity returns alone to stay with her, she realises he plans to marry someone else. Mrs Todgers is aware of Mercy's plight and gladly gives her sanctuary when she visits. One of her lodgers becomes betrothed to Charity, but no wedding takes place.

Toodle, Polly

Wet-nurse for baby Paul in *Dombey and Son*, she is re-named Richards by Paul's father, who dismisses her after Florence is lost in an unsavoury district. Her eldest son Biler, or Rob the Grinder, has been put into a charity school by Dombey, with unfortunate results. She is asked for by young Paul on his deathbed, and returns later to tend the sick and bankrupt Dombey in his empty home.

Toodle, Rob

Rob the Grinder, or Biler, in *Dombey and Son*, is Polly Toodle's eldest child, who falls into low company and acts as an informer for Carker. A miserable, whining and quite deceitful boy, he is finally given a situation with the trusting Miss Tox, though there seems little evidence of his reform.

Mr Toots, illustrated for *Dombey and Son*.

Toots, Mr

Head boy at Doctor Blimber's school in *Dombey and Son*, and a big, gormless fellow into the bargain. He takes a liking to the tiny Paul, and aids him when he can. After Paul's death, and in an inspired move, he brings the dog Diogenes from the school for Florence, with whom he is smitten. The perpetually good-natured Toots is usually on hand when assistance is needed, and after he gets over Florence's marriage to Walter, he weds Susan Nipper.

Tox, Lucretia

A good friend of Louisa Chick in *Dombey and Son*, she assists in caring for baby Paul, and is encouraged by Louisa to look hopefully at the widowed Dombey. When he marries Edith Granger she is ostracised by Louisa and the Dombeys, but she retains a kindly interest in the family, and helps Polly to tend the ruined man.

Traddles, Thomas

The simple, unaffected fellow-pupil of David Copperfield at Salem House school, the luckless Traddles is generally in trouble through no fault of his own, and mostly provides a lighter aspect to the story. David later meets him again in London, when he is lodging with the Micawbers and reading for the Bar. He is engaged over many years to "the dearest girl in the world", Sophy Crewler, "a curate's daughter, one of ten, down in Devonshire", and eventually progresses sufficiently to marry her. He becomes a steady, reliable lawyer, and assists in the exposure of Uriah Heep very competently. It is as well that he is easygoing, for his house is forever filled with a selection of Sophy's sisters.

Trent, Grandfather

The old proprietor of the Old Curiosity Shop, and selfish grandfather of Little Nell, whom he sends to Quilp to borrow money for his secret and obsessive gambling at cards. Driven by a feverish aim of accumulating wealth, ostensibly for Nell, he falls ever deeper into debt, until Quilp sells him up. Helpless and impractical, the feckless Trent flees from the shop with Nell, and they wander through the Midlands, evading the pursuing Quilp.

The despicable old man not only steals money from his own granddaughter, but intends to steal from the good-natured Mrs Jarley, Nell's employer, until thwarted by Nell who insists on their moving on.

Only when they have reached the sanctuary of their final dwelling place, where they tend the church and

churchyard, does there arise in old Trent any solicitude for Nell's welfare. By then it is too late – her health is broken. After her death the old man pines away and dies at her grave.

ABOVE: William Lugg as Grandfather Trent and Mabel Poulton as Little Nell, 1921.
RIGHT: Edith Evans as the redoubtable Betsey Trotwood, in *David Copperfield*, 1969.

Trent, Nell

The central figure in the story of *The Old Curiosity Shop*. "A small and delicate child of much sweetness of disposition", Little Nell lives with her aged, weak-willed Grandfather Trent in the muddled clutter of the shop. The evil Quilp sells Trent up, and he and Nell flee from the premises during the night. After this misfortune the book chronicles their wanderings and adventures as they are pursued by Quilp and searched for by Trent's brother. Nell has long been her grandfather's housekeeper and minder, and the demands this makes on her, together with the strain of incessant travelling on foot, and of seeking sustenance, soon tell on the frail child, whose devotion to the irresponsible old man continues to the end.

Harrowing scenes of illness and death were frequent ingredients of Victorian fiction and journalism, and child mortality was quite familiar to the reading public of Dicken's own time, but his depiction of the ailing and dying Nell moved his readers to great emotional extremes. She may well be regarded as the most celebrated of his child victims.

The story was the means of reversing the decline in the public's interest in the ill-conceived *Master Humphrey's Clock*, which ended up as the framework in which both this and *Barnaby Rudge* first appeared.

Trotter, Job

The unctuous servant and accomplice of Jingle in *The Pickwick Papers*. Trotter seems to have been the only person to have bested the sharp-witted Sam Weller, with his wily setting-up of the embarrassing predicament at the Westgate Ladies Seminary. Yet Trotter remains supremely loyal to his fellow scoundrel Jingle, and suffers with him in the Fleet Prson until they are both saved and redeemed by Pickwick's benevolence.

Job's ability to emphasise his false sincerity with tears infuriates Sam. "Wenever i catches hold o' that there melan-cholly chap with the black hair, if I don't bring some real water into his eyes. . .my name ain't Weller".

Trotwood, Betsey

When David Copperfield is born, she was so disgusted that he was not a girl that she "vanished like a discontented fairy". She is David's great-aunt, and the only person he can turn to when he runs away from his miserable occupation at Murdstone & Grinby's factory. She quickly perceives how badly Murdstone has treated both David and his mother, and takes on the responsibility for the boy in joint guardianship with the amiable, yet simple Mr Dick.

She sends David to a good school, and then pays for him to be articled to Jorkins & Spenlow. Her former husband sponges off her, she loses her money, and moves in with David in London. Her acceptance of his various situations, and her constant devotion and support, enable him eventually to become financially

independent. When the scoundrel Heep is exposed by Micawber and Traddles, she discovers that she is not ruined after all, and is able to return to her home in Dover. "I have been a grumpy, frumpy, wayward sort of a woman, a good many years. I still am, and I always shall be", she asserts to David, but in fact she is one of the most tender-hearted and kindest old dragons imaginable. She is said to be based in part on Mary Strong of Broadstairs, who was convinced that she had a divine right to drive off with a broom any donkeys who ventured in front of her sea-front cottage.

Tulkinghorn, Mr

The deep, cunning lawyer in *Bleak House*, who acts for the Dedlock family and estate. He slowly gleans information as to Lady Dedlock's past indiscretion, and seeks to influence her, but he has misjudged his intended victim, who is resigned to the eventual outcome of his machinations. The night before he intends to divulge the scandal to Sir Leicester Dedlock, he is shot dead by a neurotic former maid of Lady Dedlock.

Peter Vaughn as Tulkinghorn in a 1985 stage version of *Bleak House*.

Tupman, Tracy

The rather older and more amply built of the three companions of Mr Pickwick. Tupman still has the heart and aspirations of a young lover, and makes good progress in wooing Rachael Wardle, until he is hoodwinked by Jingle, whereupon

Alexander Gauge as Tupman and Kathleen Harrison as Mrs Bardell, 1952.

he absents himself with the intention of departing from this world. His companions find him at Cobham with his other great love – a pile of food.

Twinkleton, Miss

Proprietress of the genteel Nuns' House academy in *Edwin Drood*, where Rosa Bud and Helena Landless are taught. She is the essence of propriety, and agrees to stay with Rosa in London after Rosa has fled from Cloisterham.

Twist, Oliver

Born and raised in a parish workhouse, Oliver goes to work for Sowerberry, the undertaker, whence he runs away to London and is recruited by the Artful Dodger for Fagin's gang of thieves and pickpockets. His subsequent befriending by Mr Brownlow, recapture by the gang and eventual reunion with Brownlow and members of his rightful family are all part of one of the best-known of Dickens's books. Dramatists have seized on the highly emotional melodrama of the story, and have made a vast number of stage, film and television adaptations.

Apart from telling a compelling tale, Dickens was campaigning indirectly against the oppressive workhouse and orphanage systems of his time, and exposing a part of the grim underworld that enveloped so many of the poor and submerged of Victorian society. His growing skill as a writer enabled him to carry his readers through the various flaws – Oliver's astonishing gentility, despite a total orphanage upbringing; the far-fetched coincidences by which all his kindly friends prove to be related to him; the absurdity of maintaining that Oliver would in no way be corrupted by his experiences.

Many of the vividly-drawn characters in the story are now universally known. Almost alone, Oliver is a passive figure, tantamount to a nonentity.

BELOW: Miss Twinkleton's Academy. Ethel Griffiths (second left) as Miss Twinkleton, *Edwin Drood* 1935.
RIGHT: Mark Lester asks for more, *Oliver!*, 1969.

V

Varden, Dolly

The vain and giddy daughter of Gabriel, the locksmith in *Barnaby Rudge*. She seems not to know her own mind where men are concerned, and while Joe Willet has set his heart on her, she appears to favour the coachmaker, but nothing comes of it. She actually cares for Joe, but is too coquettish to show it, and he leaves for the army. The apprentice Simon Tappertit also fancies her, and delights in having her as a prisoner when the Gordon Riots begin, for she has been a companion to Emma Haredale at the Warren, and both girls are captured there. Rescue is finally effected by Joe and Edward Chester, and a chastened Dolly opens her heart to Joe, whom she marries. Her name was subsequently used to define a type of women's clothing, and a type of hat.

The vain Dolly Varden from *Barnaby Rudge*.

Varden, Gabriel

The genial locksmith in *Barnaby Rudge*, and father of the coquettish Dolly. His recalcitrant apprentice Simon Tappertit is the cause of Varden's premises being ransacked when the Gordon Rioters want Varden to undo the lock of the great door of Newgate Prison. Varden's valiant refusal brings him near to being killed by the rioters, but he is rescued by Joe Willet and Edward Chester, who take him and his wife to rescue Dolly and Emma Haredale. None of his experiences lessen his benevolence.

Varden, Martha

The still-attractive wife of the locksmith, Gabriel in *Barnaby Rudge*. She is incited by the shrewish Miss Miggs to moody and capricious behaviour towards her husband and daughter – "a temper tolerably certain to make everybody more or less uncomfortable". She changes her attitude after the events of the riots and the safe return of Gabriel and Dolly, and finally rids them of the intolerable Miggs.

Veneering, Anastasia

Wife of Hamilton in *Our Mutual Friend*, and hostess at their lavish dinner table. Her only contribution of significance is to have accumulated much jewellery, on which the Veneerings live after their bankruptcy.

Veneering, Hamilton

The newly-rich Veneerings are high in Society in *Our Mutual Friend*, and give endless dinner parties to countless people, all of whom are their dearest and oldest friends in the world. This enables Veneering to become an MP for a rotten borough. In the commentary which the dinner parties provide, other characters in the story are measured and found wanting by Veneering standards – until Veneering himself becomes bankrupt.

Vengeance, The

Close companion and fighting comrade of Therese Defarge in *A Tale of Two Cities*. She rejoices in the revolution, and is a regular spectator at the executions, where she keeps a place for Mme Defarge. At the end, it is not filled.

Venus, Mr

The bone-articulator and taxidermist in *Our Mutual Friend* who becomes involved in Silas Wegg's plot to deprive Boffin of his wealth and fortune. However, Venus recants, and informs Boffin of what is afoot.

Verisopht, Lord Frederick

The young nobleman in *Nicholas Nickleby* whom Ralph Nickleby plans to fleece by luring him into debt with the assistance of the offensive Sir Mulberry Hawk. Very taken with Kate Nickleby, Verisopht reproaches Hawk for refusing to identify himself to Nicholas, and later quarrels violently with Hawk over his scheme to have Nicholas waylaid. The quarrel ends in a duel and Verisopht is killed.

W

Wade, Miss

The fiercely independent young Englishwoman in *Little Dorrit*, who travels alone, and tersely rejects all offers of assistance and friendship. She encourages the hapless Tattycoram to desert the Meagles family, and rebuffs all approaches for help from Clennam and Meagles on other matters. She is left full of hatred and torment.

Wardle, Emily

Daughter of Mr Wardle of Dingley Dell in *The Pickwick Papers*. When her affection of Mr Snodgrass, and his for her, is finally revealed to both her unsuspecting father and Mr Pickwick; the latter arranges for them to be married from his new house in Dulwich.

Wardle, Isabella

Daughter of Mr Wardle of Dingley Dell in *The Pickwick Papers*. Between the visits of the Pickwickians, her marriage to Mr Trundle is arranged, and the wedding takes place just prior to the celebrated "Good-Humoured" Christmas. "Mr Pickwick was the first who saluted the bride, and in so doing he threw over her neck a rich gold watch and chain".

Wardle, Mr

The jovial yeoman-farmer of Manor Farm, Dingley Dell, in *The Pickwick Papers*. A firm friend of the Pickwickians, and Mr Samuel Pickwick in particular, Wardle is the epitome of rural good nature and well-being, and is rather a remarkable creation by an acknowledged Cockney author whose best and favourite milieu was London.

Wardle's daughters Emily and Isabella marry, and his sister Rachael nearly does, each in their turn figuring in an episode of the Pickwickians' excursions, but it is the Christmas celebrations at Wardle's farmhouse that form the earliest manifestation of Dickens's popularisation of the Christmas season.

Wardle, Mrs

Mother of the farmer-host of Manor Farm in *The Pickwick Papers*. The old lady suffers from selective deafness, and declines to hear anything at all when she is in a bad humour, even when her ear-trumpet is applied, and even when Mr Pickwick endeavours to charm her. Her ill-humour is generally short-lived, and she joins in card games and dancing when prevailed upon to do so.

Wardle, Rachael

Sister of Mr Wardle of Dingley Dell in *The Pickwick Papers*. The foolish Rachael is easily duped by the unscrupulous Jingle into believing that Tupman is enamoured of her niece Emily rather than her, and agrees to elope with Jingle. After a wild chase, the couple are confronted by Wardle, Pickwick and Perker, and Rachael refuses to return home. "Lady's free to act as she pleases", says Jingle, "more than one-and-twenty". "More than one-and-forty!" retorts Wardle. Her immediate betrayal by Jingle for money leaves her devastated, and she disappears from the story.

Rachel Wardle (left) and her niece Emily, from *The Pickwick Papers*.

''Christmas eve at Mr Wardle's'', as drawn
by Phiz.

Wegg, Silas

The wooden-legged ballad-seller in *Our Mutual Friend*, who is hired by the newly-rich Boffin to read to him, and who is installed in the Boffin house by the dust yard, where he speculates on the contents of the dust mounds. Finding a will by the late John Harmon, he attempts to coerce Boffin into parting with his fortune, but Boffin and Rokesmith are too smart for him.

Silas Wegg, the wooden-legged ballad seller in *Our Mutual Friend*.

Weller, Sam

Next to Mr Pickwick himself, Sam Weller provides the foremost continuing thread through the diverse episodes of *The Pickwick Papers*, and the development of the relationship between these two is the most enduring and touching aspect of the book. Once Sam comes on the scene, Pickwick has the assurance of some practical assistance in his various troubles, instead of the helpless buffoonery of his three travelling companions.

Sam's early years are succinctly recounted to Pickwick by his father,

Tony Weller: "I took a good deal o' pains with his eddication, sir; let him run in the streets when he was very young, and shift for hisself. It's the only way to make a boy sharp".

"I worn't always a boots, sir," Sam confides to his new employer. "I wos a vagginer's boy once . . . When I wos first pitched neck and crop into the world to

Sam Weller and his father Tony, illustrated by Fred Barnard in *The Pickwick Papers*.

play at leapfrog with its troubles . . . I wos a carrier's boy at startin'; then a vagginer's, then a helper, then a boots. Now I'm a gen'l'm'ns servant. I shall be a gen'l'm'n myself one of these days, perhaps with a pipe in my mouth and a summer-house in the back garden".

Although the streetwise Sam proves invaluable in rescuing Mr Pickwick from a variety of awkward and embarrassing situations, even he is shown to be fallible when he is duped by the lugubrious Job Trotter, but his view of Trotter is modified when they later meet in the Fleet Prison. Trotter's appreciation of Pickwick's benevolent forgiveness is capped by Sam's eulogy: "I never heerd, mind you, nor read of in story-books, nor see in picters, any angel in tights and gaiters", says Sam proudly, "not even in spectacles, as I remember . . . but mark my vords, Job Trotter he's a regular thorough-bred angel for all that".

It is seldom realised that the disappointing and dwindling sales of the first few numbers of *The Pickwick Papers* were transformed into a resounding success by the introduction of the character Sam Weller – a salutary lesson which Charles Dickens seems never to have forgotten. In this, his first piece of sustained writing, Dickens was able to use various interpolated stories to make up the required number of pages per month, but the main thread, once created, was the companionship of Mr Pickwick and Sam.

Weller, Tony

Father of Sam Weller in *The Pickwick Papers*, and a driver of long-distance coaches. Perpetually issuing warnings against the dangers of marrying a "widder", Tony Weller sees himself as a terrible example of such folly, but the widow he has married eventually dies, and he remains well clear of matrimony thereafter. A brilliantly-drawn character by Dickens, Mr Weller senior figures in one of the side issues of the book – the diverting episode involving the second Mrs Weller and Mr Stiggins. It should be noted that Mrs Weller is referred to throughout as Sam's "mother-in-law", a Victorian usage long since replaced by the term "stepmother".

Wemmick, John

In *Great Expectations*, clerk to the lawyer Jaggers, to whom he is completely loyal. "A dry man, rather short in stature, with a square wooden face, whose expression seemed to have been chipped out with a dull-edged chisel". He befriends Pip, and takes him to his bizarre home in Walworth, where also lives his "Aged Parent". Wemmick is the agent through

Ivor Barnard (left) as Jagger's clerk, Wemmick.

whom Pip pieces together much of Estella's history, and is of constant help to Pip, even though his advice regarding portable property is disastrously ignored.

Westlock, John
Pupil of Seth Pecksniff in *Martin Chuzzlewit*. At the beginning of the story Westlock leaves Pecksniff with harsh words, to the distress of Tom Pinch, who is very friendly with Westlock but cannot understand or accept his criticism of Pecksniff.

Westlock prospers in London, and is a true friend to Tom when he is discharged by Pecksniff. Westlock discovers the sick Lewsome, aids his recovery, and reveals his secret of having supplied Jonas Chuzzlewit with the means of poisoning his own father. In the meantime he has met and fallen in love with Tom's sister Ruth, and, with old Martin's assistance, marries her, having enabled old Martin to confront Jonas with the evidence of Lewsome and Chuffey.

Whisker
Dickens succeeded in creating a real animal character in the Garlands' pony in *The Old Curiosity Shop*. Whisker would neither stop nor start, nor steer properly, until handled by Kit, whose special friend he became. When Kit was imprisoned he would suffer only Barbara to feed him. "The pony preserved his character for independence and principle down to the last moment of his life."

Wickfield, Agnes
When David Copperfield lodges at Mr Wickfield's to attend Doctor Strong's school, Agnes is her father's dutiful companion and housekeeper. A dear friend to David, she tries in vain to warn him against Steerforth's influence, and confesses her fears of Heep's power over her father. David's attachment to her is more like that of a brother, and she remains a firm and loyal friend. Devoted to her father, she becomes aware of Heep's desire to marry her.

After Heep's departure, and the

Susan Hampshire as the devoted Agnes Wickfield, *David Copperfield*, 1969.

settling of her father's affairs, she opens a small school in the former business premises, and when David returns from abroad, they marry.

"Mr Wickfield and his partner wait upon my aunt", *David Copperfield*.

Wickfield, Mr

David Copperfield lodges at Mr Wickfield's house in Canterbury while at school. There he observes the growing influence of Uriah Heep over Wickfield, who is cared for by his devoted daughter Agnes. Wickfield is a friend of Miss Trotwood, and is believed to have ruined her by unwise investment, but the real culprit is Heep.

Through forgery and false accounting, Heep convinces Wickfield that he is responsible for serious defalcation, but Wickfield is rescued by the efforts of Micawber and Traddles to uncover the truth.

Wilfer, Bella

Elder daughter of Reginald Wilfer in *Our Mutual Friend*, and a beautiful, capricious girl. Long burdened by the expectation of having to marry John Harmon by the terms of the will, she is thrilled to escape from the tiny, modest, family home to live with the Boffins, once Harmon Jnr is presumed dead. She describes herself as mercenary, and certainly appears so, as well as spoiled, but her natural charm and good nature overcome these faults, and although she has always hoped to marry money, her observations of its corruption of the Boffins, and her indignation at their hard and unfair treatment of Rokesmith, change her views.

She indiscreetly disloses to a supposed friend that Rokesmith has proposed to her, and when this information is deliberately passed to the Boffins, Bella is appalled to see that it is used as an excuse for discharging him. She rounds on the Boffins in disgust, and leaves. Rokesmith follows her, and they are soon wed, for she has learned the lesson which all along has been plotted for her. But she does not learn of Rokesmith's true identity until later, and discovers that she has not only married money after all, but she has also married John Harmon.

Wilfer, Mrs

Wife of Reginald in *Our Mutual Friend*. Totally unreasonable and unapproachable, she is a form of non-violent Mrs Joe Gargery, and is perpetually affronted, no matter what the course of action that anyone adopts. Even the great good fortune that befalls Bella and her husband fails to soften her very much.

Wilfer, Reginald

The docile, cherubic father of the Wilfer family in *Our Mutual Friend*. Downtrodden by his wife, but ever cheerful, he delights in his daughter Bella's good fortune in being taken in by the Boffins, and she returns his great love. He is a humble clerk at Veneering's business, and participates in Bella's secret wedding to Rokesmith. Later he becomes secretary to the new Harmon/Boffin household, thus avoiding the ruin of the Veneering crash.

The eclectic Wilfer family from *Our Mutual Friend*.

Willet, Joe

In *Barnaby Rudge* Joe is the resentful son of John Willet, who treats Joe abominably: "There never was an unfortunate young fellow so bullied, badgered, worried, fretted and brow-beaten; so constantly beset, or made so tired of his life, as poor Joe Willet". Small wonder then that Joe leaves, and enlists as a soldier. He loses an arm in the fighting in America, and returns in time to help rescue Emma Haredale and his beloved Dolly Varden from the hands of the rioters. His humble adoration of Dolly finally gives her the courage to respond accordingly, and they marry and take over the Maypole farm.

Willet, John

"A burly, large-headed man with a fat face, which betokened profound obstinacy and slowness of apprehension, combined with a very strong reliance on his own merits", Old John is the first character to appear in *Barnaby Rudge*. His incomprehension of his son's manhood drives Joe away from the Maypole at Chigwell, where John is the slow-witted landlord, very careful with money. Shocked by the damage to the Maypole caused by the rioters, he later returns and is reconciled to Joe's marriage to Dolly.

Winkel, Nathaniel

Winkle is seemingly the token sportsman in *The Pickwick Papers*, because the original idea, by the ill-fated illustrator Robert Seymour, was for a series of adventures of Cockney sportsmen to back up Seymour's projected illustrations. Dickens had other ideas, however, which prevailed over those of Seymour, who only illustrated one-and-a-half of the 24 monthly parts of the book before he died at his own hand.

So Winkle is portrayed by Dickens as an aspiring but inept sportsman. On his first sporting outing he merely succeeds in wounding Tupman. Shortly after, Wardle asks if he is a cricketer. "At any other time Mr Winkle would have replied in the affirmative. He felt the delicacy of his situation, and modestly replied 'No'". Pickwick deliberately emphasises the delicacy of the situation: "I . . . am delighted to view any sports which may be safely indulged in, and in which the impotent effects of unskilled people do not endanger human life".

The dithering Winkle, very nearly a participant in a duel with Doctor Slammer following Jingle's intransigence, is transformed when he meets Arabella Allen at the Dingley Dell Christmas festivities. His resolve is such that they subsequently marry without the consent of Winkle's stern father, and when the dreaded encounter with his father takes place, Nathaniel at last stands up for himself: "I am very sorry to have done anything which has lessened your affection for me . . . but I have no reason to be ashamed of having this lady for my wife, nor you of having her for a daughter".

Witherfield, Miss

The middle-aged lady in yellow curl-papers into whose bedroom Mr Pickwick inadvertently strays. She is the betrothed of Peter Magnus. The harmless incident leads to a serious encounter with a magistrate, and later proves a damning piece of evidence let slip by Winkle in the Bardell versus Pickwick trial.

Woodcourt, Allan

The young surgeon in *Bleak House*, who spends much time tending to poor people, during which he first meets Esther Summerson. She is gradually attracted to him, but remains loyal to her guardian. Woodcourt tends the dying Jo, and at Esther's earnest request keeps a close eye on the recalcitrant and weakening Richard Carstone. Eventually Jarndyce selflessly gives up Esther to Woodcourt.

Wrayburn, Eugene

The cynical and insolent barrister in *Our Mutual Friend*, who has no regard for anyone until he encounters Lizzie

Hexam. His pursuit of her seems groundless, since they are so far apart on the social scale, which troubles Lizzie, but not him. He is confronted by Charley Hexam and Bradley Headstone about Lizzie, and realises Headstone's interest. He then engages in a despicable deception of Headstone, leading him for miles, night after night, since Headstone believes that Wrayburn knows Lizzie's whereabouts. Wrayburn eventually gains that knowledge by his unscrupulous treatment of Jenny Wren's drunken father, and finds Lizzie. Headstone has continued to trail him, and mounts a murderous attack on him. Wrayburn's

Jenny Wren lectures her drunken father in *Our Mutual Friend*.

survival is entirely due to Lizzie's great efforts: "She would have done well to have turned me over with her foot that night when I lay bleeding to death, and to have spat in my dastard face". And well she might have done, but instead she marries him.

Wren, Jenny

Real name Fanny Cleaver, in *Our Mutual Friend*. The dolls' dressmaker is a steadfast friend to Lizzie Hexam, who lodges with her for a time until she moves to avoid her pursuers. Jenny will not reveal her whereabouts, but her drunken father does to Wrayburn. Jenny is later summoned to Wrayburn's sick-bed at his request, where she helps to nurse him, and witnesses his wedding to Lizzie.

Acknowledgments

The publisher would like to thank Ron Callow of Design 23 for designing this book; Suzanne O'Farrell for picture research; Simon Shelmerdine, the production manager; and Judith Millidge, the editor. We should also like to thank the following individuals and agencies for permission to reproduce photographic material:

British Film Institute, pages: 2(top left and right, centre left and right, and bottom right), 9(both), 10(top right and centre), 11(top and bottom), 12(top and bottom), 13(bottom), 14, 17(bottom), 20, 21(bottom), 25, 27, 30(top), 31, 33, 34(both), 35, 36, 39, 41, 42, 43, 47, 48(both), 49, 51, 52, 53(top), 54-55(both), 56(bottom), 57, 58, 60, 61, 69, 72, 73, 74, 77, 79, 80, 84, 85, 86-87, 90, 92, 93, 94, 95(both), 96, 98(top), 100-101, 102, 103(all three), 106, 106-107, 110, 116, 117, 118, 122-123, 124(both), 128, 130, 130-131, 132, 133, 134, 135, 142, 143, 145, 146, 147, 154, 155.
Dickens House Museum, pages: 16, 18, 21(top), 22(top), 24, 40(below), 50, 88, 127, 129, 138, 141, 150, 152, 156, 157, 159.
Donald Cooper/Photostage, pages 13(top), 36-37, 104-105.
Eastern Daily Press, page 109(top).
Granada Television, pages: 11(centre), 19, 65, 66-67.
Grantham Journal/Melton and Rutland Journal, pages 40(top), 144.
Hulton-Deutsch, pages: 1, 3, 5, 6(both), 7(top right and bottom), 8(both), 15, 17(top), 22(bottom), 26, 30-31, 32, 38(top), 44, 45, 46, 53(bottom), 56(top), 59, 62, 63, 64, 68, 75, 78, 89, 99, 105, 109(bottom), 111, 112, 113, 114-115, 119, 120, 125, 126, 136, 137, 139(both), 148, 151, 152, 153, 156.
Life File, pages: 7(top left/Andrew Ward), 10(bottom/Andrew Ward).
Michael Pointer, pages: 2(bottom left), 11(centre), 12(centre), 19, 23, 38(bottom), 40(top), 65, 66-67, 71, 81, 86, 91, 98(bottom), 108, 144.